U. S. SUPREME COURT: SIX DECISIONS THAT CHANGED AMERICA

A Compilation of PowerPoint Presentations

Robert A. Frick

U. S. Supreme Court:
Six Decisions That Changed America

A Compilation of PowerPoint Presentations

by
Robert A. Frick, Ed.D.

ISBN-10: 171712660X
ISBN-13: 978-1717126603

Printed in the United States of America
by
CreateSpace, an Amazon.com Company

Available from Amazon.com and other retail outlets

DEDICATION

This book is dedicated to Dr. H. C. Hudgins, Jr.,
Scholar, Professor, Friend.

ACKNOWLEDGMENTS

First, I acknowledge and thank Dr. H.C. Hudgins, my law professor at Temple University during my doctoral program. His dynamic classroom presentation style and his deep knowledge of the intricacies of constitutional law were both informative and inspirational. It was he who planted the seed of interest in the law that blossomed into my life-long curiosity and study.

More importantly, I acknowledge and thank my wife Bonnie for her encouragement, many hours of research, and a seemingly endless task of editing and proofreading to put my PowerPoint presentations into book form. While these efforts played no small part in the creation of this treatise, the most critical element that she supplied was her honesty in critiquing my work. When I was verbose, she told me. When my story was confusing, she told me. When my conclusions were not clear, she told me. Thanks, partner.

CONTENTS

U.S. SUPREME COURT: SIX DECISIONS THAT CHANGED AMERICA

INTRODUCTION

Oyez is a traditional interjection said two or three times in succession to introduce the opening of a court of law, especially in Great Britain. The interjection is also traditionally used by town criers to attract the attention of the public to public proclamations. It is a form of the Anglo-Norman word *oyer* meaning "to hear."

OYEZ! OYEZ! OYEZ!

The term is still used by the Supreme Court of the United States. At the beginning of each session, the marshal of the Court announces: *The Honorable, the Chief Justice and the Associate Justices of the Supreme Court of the United States. Oyez! Oyez! Oyez! All persons having business before the Honorable, the Supreme Court of the United States, are admonished to draw near and give their attention, for the Court is now sitting. God save the United States and this Honorable Court.*

The Supreme Court was established in Article III, Section 1, of the Constitution of the United States of America.

ARTICLE III, SECTION 1

The judicial power of the United States shall be vested in one Supreme Court, and in such inferior courts as the

9

Congress may from time to time ordain and establish. The judges, both of the Supreme and inferior courts, shall, at stated times, receive for their services, a compensation, which shall not be diminished during their continuance in office.

ARTICLE III, SECTION 2

The judicial power shall extend to all cases, in law and equity, arising under this Constitution, the laws of the United States, and treaties made, or which shall be made, under their authority. . . .

AUTHORITY

The Supreme Court has ultimate appellate jurisdiction over the following:
- All federal courts
- All state courts where federal law is involved
- Original jurisdiction over a small range of cases

Decisions of the U. S. Supreme Court are final.

HISTORY OF THE COURT

As designed by federal statutes, the Supreme Court is composed of a Chief Justice and eight Associate Justices.

The first Supreme Court–as nominated by President George Washington–was composed of six members: Chief Justice John Jay and Associate Justices John Rutledge; William Cushing; James Wilson; John Blair, Jr.; and James Iredell.

The Constitution, ratified in 1788, does not specify the number of Supreme Court Justices. The Judiciary Act of 1789, however, required Washington to appoint six Justices. As the nation grew in size and population over the years, the number of Justices changed to seven in 1807, to nine in 1837, and to ten in 1863. In 1869, the Circuit Judges Act returned the number of seats to nine, where it has since remained.

Franklin Roosevelt attempted to expand the number of Justices in 1937. His plan called for another Justice to be appointed when a seated judge reached the age of 70 and did not retire. The maximum number of Justices under FDR's plan would have been 15. While the President stated that it would ease the workload on older judges, Congress defeated it, seeing it as an effort to "pack the Court" to get New Deal programs approved quickly. By 1941, as a result of attrition, FDR had appointed seven Justices.

According to the Constitution, the President "shall nominate, by and with the advice and consent of the Senate . . . appoint judges of the Supreme Court . . . ." Most nominees in modern times have been persons who share the same ideological views as the nominating President. The controlling political party in the Senate and a variety of advocacy groups help determine the likelihood of a nominee's success.

The term of the Supreme Court commences on the first Monday of October and continues until June or early July of the following year. Each term consists of alternating sittings and recesses of approximately two weeks. The Justices hear cases during the sittings and discuss cases and work on opinions during recesses.

Appointments to the Supreme Court are life appointments, assuming "good behavior." As of January 1, 2018, the Chief Justice of the Supreme Court receives $267,000, while Associate Justices receive $255,300.

THE OCTOBER 2017 COURT

- John Roberts, nominated by George W. Bush in 2005 and presently serving as Chief Justice, was confirmed by a vote of 78-22.
- Anthony Kennedy, nominated by Ronald Reagan in 1988, was confirmed by a vote of 97-0.
- Clarence Thomas, nominated by George H. W. Bush in 1991, was confirmed by a vote of 52-48.
- Ruth Bader Ginsburg, nominated by William Clinton in 1993, was confirmed by a vote of 96-3.
- Stephen Breyer, nominated by William Clinton in 1994, was confirmed by a vote of 87-9.
- Samuel Alito, nominated by George W. Bush in 2006, was confirmed by a vote of 58-42.
- Sonia Sotomayor, nominated by Barack Obama in 2009, was confirmed by a vote of 68-31.
- Elena Kagan, nominated by Barack Obama in 2010, was confirmed by a vote of 63-37.
- Neil Gorsuch, nominated by Donald Trump in 2017, was confirmed by a vote of 54-45.

Five of the 2017 Justices were nominated by Republican Presidents, and four of the current Justices were nominated by Democratic Presidents.

Six Justices are male, and three are female.

One Justice is African-American (Thomas), and one is Hispanic (Sotomayor). Two Justices were born to at least one immigrant parent. Alito's parents were born in Italy, and Ginsburg's father was born in Russia.

Five Justices are Roman Catholic, and three are Jewish.

Four Justices are from New York, two from California, one from New Jersey, one from Georgia, and one from Colorado.

All nine Justices have an Ivy League education, and their average age is 67 years.

With the death of Antonin Scalia on February 13, 2016, a vacancy was created on the Court. Although President Obama had eleven months remaining in his term, the Republican-controlled Senate would not hold confirmation hearings to consider nominations from what they called a "lame-duck President."

Had President Obama been able to successfully nominate someone to take Justice Scalia's place, the Court would have had five Justices nominated by a Democratic President and four nominated by a Republican President. Instead, with the nomination of Neil Gorsuch by President Trump, no change occurred in the political balance of the Court.

IN THE WORDS OF WILLIAM HOWARD TAFT:

Presidents come and go,
but the Supreme Court goes on forever.

MARBURY V. MADISON (1803)

Congress does not have the power to modify the Constitution through regular legislation because the Supremacy Clause places the Constitution before the laws. In so holding, Marshall established the principle of judicial review, i.e., the power to declare a law unconstitutional.

~ OYEZ

INTRODUCTION

In the presidential election of 1800, John Adams, the incumbent President of the United States, finished third in the balloting. Thomas Jefferson and Aaron Burr tied for the office, each receiving 73 electoral votes, while Adams' tally was 65. Eventually, because of Alexander Hamilton's manipulation, Jefferson was declared President. Adams and many other Federalists were convinced that the government that had been established would crumble under Jefferson and the Democratic-Republicans. The Democratic-Republicans vowed to end the reign of the Federalists, whom they perceived as aristocratic Anglophiles.

JUDICIARY ACT OF 1789

Officially titled "An Act to Establish the Judicial Courts of the United States," the legislation was designed to set up the organization of the U.S. Federal Court System that had been sketched in general terms in the Constitution. The Act provided a three-part judiciary comprised of District courts, Circuit courts, and the Supreme Court, plus the structure and jurisdiction of each branch. The Act also created the office of Attorney General, making it part of the cabinet.

ADAMS' LAST ACTS

As written by David McCullough: *For weeks Adams had been exercising his presidential prerogative to fill government positions of all kinds, including some for friends and relatives.*

The lame-duck President paid particular attention to his court appointments during his last month in office, and nearly all of his appointments were Federalists. Adams' thinking was that although the Democratic-Republicans controlled the Executive Office and Congress, the courts would be beyond Jefferson's control and a stronghold of Federalism. According to Historian John Garraty, Adams believed that "he was saving the republic itself."

To help Adams in his effort to make the judiciary a Federalist stronghold, the lame-duck Congress passed the Judiciary Act of 1801. This new Act relieved Supreme Court Justices from Circuit Court duty, increased the number of Circuit Court judges, and created a considerable number of minor judicial posts.

In this same time period between the election and the inauguration, Adams replaced the aged Chief Justice Oliver Ellsworth with John Marshall, a forceful opponent of Jeffersonian principles. Confirmed by the Senate in January, Marshall also continued to serve as Secretary of State.

JOHN MARSHALL

John Marshall was born in 1755 on the Virginia frontier, one of 15 children born to Thomas Marshall and Mary Randolph. As a descendant of the Randolph Family, he was related to his oft-times opponent Thomas Jefferson, a man whom "he distrusted greatly."

As a child, Marshall received little education, but he possessed a "quick mind." When the Revolutionary War broke out, Marshall was inspired to join the fighting by his father's good friend, General George Washington. Distinguishing himself in battle, he also served as Washington's chief legal officer.

Following his involvement in the war, Marshall opted to study law, and he attended a series of lectures by George Wythe at the College of William & Mary, "the only formal education he would receive." In 1780, he was admitted to the Virginia Bar and began his own law practice.

The roles that Marshall played in government were numerous and varied, first representing Fauquier County, Virginia, in the General Assembly and subsequently serving as a magistrate presiding over small criminal and civil court cases. Here he earned the reputation of being a "fair and honest man who communicated clearly and based his decisions on the common good."

In 1788, he served as a delegate to the state committee to ratify the United States Constitution. Turning down an invitation to join the U.S. Supreme Court in 1798, he served instead as a diplomat to France in what was eventually called the XYZ Affair. Elected to a seat in the House of Representatives in 1799, John Marshall was appointed Secretary of State by Adams in 1800. As

Secretary of State, the most important task that Marshall completed was overseeing the movement of the federal capital from Philadelphia to Washington, D.C.

During the last sixteen days of his administration, Adams proceeded to fill 67 newly created vacancies, completing their commissions at approximately 9:00 p.m. on March 3, 1801, his last day in office. All had been approved by the Senate. Forty-two of these federal positions were Justices of the Peace for the District of Columbia. Each of the completed commissions was then delivered to the State Department where Marshall was to affix the Great Seal of the United States to each and see that they were delivered to the appointees.

As opined by historian John Garrity: *Marshall, a Virginian with something of the southerner's easygoing carelessness about detail, failed to complete this routine task.* While he did place the Seal on each one, he failed to have them delivered.

JEFFERSON'S RESPONSE

Jefferson was inaugurated on March 4, 1801. His newly appointed Secretary of State was James Madison. Days after his inauguration, Jefferson found a stack of letters on a table at the State Department. When the President realized what they were, he forbade their delivery. Then, Jefferson created a list of Justices of the Peace and instructed the Attorney General to notify them of their appointments. The list was reduced from Adams' forty-two appointments to thirty, twenty-three of whom were Adams' men. Only seven were Jefferson's people.

JEFFERSON'S PLAN

Once in office, Jefferson conferred with Madison, and their plan was to try to abolish the new system of circuit courts as created by the lame-duck Congress in early 1801. In January of 1802, a bill to repeal that legislation was introduced in Congress and passed by the Democratic-Republican majority to repeal that legislation. The relatively newly appointed circuit court judges now deposed, petitioned Congress for "relief," but their request was summarily dismissed. The deposed judges argued that since their appointments were for life, the repeal act was, therefore, unconstitutional. They threatened to appeal to the Supreme Court.

Marshall, certainly no friend of the administration, was prepared to declare the eliminating of the circuit court judges as unconstitutional, but none of the deposed judges would file an appeal to the Court. To prevent Chief Justice Marshall and the Supreme Court from becoming involved in the issue, Jefferson got a bill passed through Congress that abolished the June 1802 term of the Court, setting the next session to begin the second Monday of February 1803.

ENTER THE PLAINTIFF, WILLIAM MARBURY

William Marbury, an ambitious man, was one of the nineteen not appointed by Jefferson. Born on November 7, 1762, Marbury came from a wealthy Maryland family that owned a plantation in Charles County. As a young, opportunistic man in the 1780s, Marbury's first public position was Deputy Tax Collector in Annapolis, Maryland. In addition to becoming a wealthy man, he became part of important social circles, "rubbing elbows with the rich and famous like Alexander Hamilton and

John Adams." When the time came for Marbury to choose to be part of the Federalist or Anti-federalist camp, he chose the Federalists. Professionally, he played an important role in the banking industry of Washington, D.C.

ENTER THE DEFENDANT, JAMES MADISON

The position that would have been responsible for the delivery of the commissions was that of the Secretary of State. James Madison had replaced John Marshall in that position, and under the direction of Jefferson, Madison refused to deliver the commission to Marbury.

James Madison was born to a wealthy planter in 1751 at Montpelier, the ancestral home of the Madison Family in Orange County, Virginia. A graduate of the College of New Jersey (Princeton), Madison was initially supportive of the Federalist cause, writing much of the Constitution and aiding Alexander Hamilton in developing *The Federalist Papers*.

During the years Washington was President, Madison served in Congress and communicated regularly with his friend, Thomas Jefferson, the Secretary of State. Jefferson had recently returned from his years in France where he had gained an admiration for French culture that he shared with Madison, his protégé. Through his friendship with Jefferson, Madison became less and less a supporter of the Federalist cause and more and more a follower of the Jeffersonian philosophy that eventually became identified as the Democratic-Republican faction. By the time John Adams became President in 1797, Madison was philosophically in the same camp as Jefferson.

THE SUIT

Although nominated for the position by President Adams, approved by the Senate, and commissioned by the hand of the outgoing President, Marbury never received his commission. Thus, Marbury went directly to the Supreme Court of the United States and filed suit against Secretary of State Madison who had refused to deliver his commission. Marbury claimed that under section 13 of the Judiciary Act of 1789, the Supreme Court had the ability to issue a mandamus that would serve as his remedy.

Definition: *Mandamus*–from the Latin meaning "We command." A mandamus is "an extraordinary writ issued from a court to an official compelling performance of a ministerial act that the law recognizes as an absolute duty, as distinct from other types of acts that may be a matter of the official's discretion."

SECTION 13

Section 13 of the Judiciary Act of 1789 states in part:
The Supreme Court shall have power to issue writs of prohibition to the district courts, when proceeding as courts of admiralty and maritime jurisdiction, and writs of mandamus, in cases warranted by the principles and usages of law, to any courts appointed, or persons holding office, under the authority of the United States.

MARSHALL'S DILEMMA

At this point, Marshall encountered two dangers.

- The Democratic-Republicans were wary of a Federalist-dominated judiciary.
- As a devoted Federalist, Marshall had the temptation to use the courts to improve the Federalist program.

The Court's authority to employ judicial review was controversial at the time the Constitution was being developed. Thus, the language in the Constitution was vague in this regard. It appeared that the suit brought by Marbury would provoke a direct confrontation between the Supreme Court and the Republican administration under the new President, Thomas Jefferson. Chief Justice Marshall's major concern by this time was that the Supreme Court had not yet established itself as a major player in the government of the country.

The role of the Supreme Court was vague as defined in the Constitution. That vagueness was the reason that the Judicial Act of 1789 had been developed and passed. The Act was designed to put "arms and legs" to the general intent that the Founding Fathers had for the Court. Since the Court had ruled on few cases and nearly all of the decisions handed down lacked any significance, it lacked prestige and did not possess the authority it holds today. An article in a prominent newspaper of the day added support to the lack of significance of the Court by referring to the role of Chief Justice as one of **sinecure**. *Sinecure* is defined as an office or position that requires little or no work and that usually provides an income.

When Marshall assumed the office of Chief Justice in 1801, the Court did not even have its own meeting room. Instead, the Court "met in the office of the clerk of the Senate, a small room on the first floor of what is now the north wing of the Capitol." Marshall believed that if the Court ordered Madison to deliver the commission to Marbury, it would be ignored by the administration. This response could have further weakened the Court. To determine the Court's response, Marshall developed three queries:

- Has the applicant a right to the commission he demands?
- If that right has been violated, do the laws of the United States afford him a remedy?
- Is the remedy a mandamus issuing from this Supreme Court?

RESPONSE TO QUERY NUMBER 1

Does Marbury have a right to the commission? The Court responded that he did.

As explained by political scientist Paul Bartholomew:
By signing the commission of Mr. Marbury, John Adams, President, appointed him a justice of the peace, and the seal of the United States affixed thereto by the Secretary of State . . . conferred on Marbury a legal right to the office for the space of five years. By indicating in his response that Marbury had the right to receive the commission properly signed by President Adams and approved by the Senate, Marshall was somewhat chastising Madison and Jefferson for denying it to the plaintiff. Jefferson's unsuccessful argument was that under English Common Law, a person did not actually get something until it was delivered.

RESPONSE TO QUERY NUMBER 2

Does the law provide a remedy for the plaintiff? It is an indisputable rule that where there is a legal right, there is legal remedy whenever that right is violated. Therefore, Marbury was due a remedy under United States law. Again, the Court's response indicated to both Madison and Jefferson that Marbury had been treated inappropriately. Marbury was due a remedy for the violation of his rights.

RESPONSE TO QUERY NUMBER 3

Is the remedy that Marbury was due a mandamus from the Supreme Court? In essence, the Court said: "Yes, Mr. Marbury, you have a right to your commission. Yes, Mr. Marbury, you deserve a remedy. But, no, Mr. Marbury, the Supreme Court is not the place to get that remedy."

MARSHALL'S RATIONALE

Marshall, writing for the Court, said that the Supreme Court has no authority to issue a mandamus to the Secretary of State, and the reason involved original jurisdiction. District and superior (circuit) courts have the responsibility to hear most cases first. This is called *original jurisdiction*. As defined by the Constitution, the Supreme Court has very limited original jurisdiction.

Under Article III, Section 2, of the Constitution, the Court's original jurisdiction is limited as follows:
In all cases affecting ambassadors, other public ministers and consuls, and those in which a State shall be party, the Supreme Court shall have original jurisdiction. In all other cases before mentioned, the Supreme Court shall have

appellate jurisdiction, both as to law and fact, with such exceptions, and under such regulations as the Congress shall make.

The claim made by Marbury was based on Section 13 of the Judiciary Act of 1789 that expanded the powers of the Court by saying that it could "issue writs of mandamus, in cases warranted by the principles and usages of law, to any courts appointed, or persons holding office, under the authority of the United States." The Constitution did not give the Court that right! Since Section 13 of the Judiciary Act of 1789 exceeded the authority defined by the Constitution, the Court declared Section 13 unconstitutional and, therefore, void. The Court had no authority to grant Marbury's request and, therefore, canceled his claim.

SIGNIFICANCE OF *MARBURY V. MADISON*

Marshall and the Court's *Marbury* decision formally declared the Constitution the "superior, paramount law" of the United States. When ordinary laws conflict with the Constitution, they must be struck down. This is the principle of *judicial review*, and the responsibility to determine the constitutionality of a law is that of the Supreme Court.

Marbury further established that it is the job of the judicial department of the United States government to interpret what the Constitution says. It is not the role of Congress. It is not the role of the President. It is the job of the Supreme Court, pure and simple.

Through *Marbury,* Marshall led the Court to be more than part of the politics of Washington, D.C. Presidents appoint–

with the confirmation of the Senate–Justices to the Supreme Court who share their opinions on controversial topics. The Constitution of the United States, however, remains the focus of the Court.

IN CONCLUSION

Thus, in 1803, the Supreme Court of the United States declared an Act of Congress to be unconstitutional.

Another 50 years would pass before the Court again declared an Act of Congress unconstitutional in *Dred Scott v. Sandford*.

DRED SCOTT V. SANDFORD (1857)

A negro, whose ancestors were imported into [the U.S.], and sold as slaves," whether enslaved or free, could not be an American citizen and therefore did not have standing to sue in federal court. . . . The Court further held that the Missouri Compromise of 1820 was unconstitutional and foreclose Congress from freeing slaves within Federal territories.

~ OYEZ

EARLY LIFE

Dred Scott was born in Southampton County, Virginia, in approximately 1795. Born a slave to slave parents, Scott, according to historian Bruce Catton, grew up illiterate and "physically frail, a man without energy." Because of his frailty, no one really wanted him as a slave. Catton wrote that he was "a liability rather than an asset."

Scott was originally the property of Peter Blow. In 1827, Blow moved first to Alabama and then to St. Louis, Missouri, taking with him his family and his chattels. Five years later, Blow died, and Scott was purchased from Blow's wife in 1833 by Dr. John Emerson, a surgeon for the United States Army. For the next two and a half years, Emerson served as the post physician for Fort Armstrong, a military base located in Illinois near the present city of Rock Island.

In 1787, the old Congress, still operating under the Articles of Confederation and Perpetual Union, passed the Northwest Ordinance. The law stated unequivocally that "slavery and involuntary servitude was prohibited in all of the American territories north and west of the Ohio River." This included the area that would eventually become the states of Ohio, Indiana, Illinois, Michigan, and Wisconsin. After the Constitution was ratified, the new Congress reaffirmed the Ordinance. Even though Illinois was a free state, Scott, however, did not claim that he was now emancipated. Likely, he just did not know that he could do so.

In 1836, Emerson was reassigned to Fort Snelling in what today is the state of Minnesota. The Missouri Compromise of 1820, which "forever prohibited" slavery in this territory, was in effect. In addition, the Wisconsin Enabling Act passed by Congress two weeks after Emerson and Scott arrived reinforced the laws of the Northwest Ordinance and declared that the laws of Michigan–where slavery was also forbidden–were in effect. Thus, the Northwest Ordinance, the Missouri Compromise, and the Wisconsin Enabling Act all indicated that Scott could have claimed his freedom. Emerson and Scott were there for two years, and, again, Scott likely did not know that he could claim emancipation.

HIS WIFE

During the two years he was at Fort Snelling, Scott met and married Harriet Robinson, the slave of Major Lawrence Taliaferro, an Indian agent. Taliaferro was also a justice of the peace, and he performed the civil ceremony. Permitting slaves to be married in a civil service was illegal in the United States at this time. Slave marriages were prohibited for three reasons.

- Legal recognition of slave marriages could prevent owners from selling one of the partners.
- A civil marriage is a contract, and slaves were not permitted to make contracts.

- Recognition of slave rights might give slaves the motivation to claim other rights.

Lawyers later indicated that the marriage was further evidence that both Major Taliaferro and Dr. Emerson believed that the two slaves were former slaves and were, in effect, free. Scott made no effort, however, to declare himself to be free.

SLAVE LIFE

In October of 1837, Dr. Emerson was sent to St. Louis, Missouri, but the Scotts remained at Fort Snelling and were rented out to other people. Technically, renting the Scotts to other people "brought slavery to a free territory," which was a clear violation of the Missouri Compromise, the Northwest Ordinance, and the Wisconsin Enabling Act.

In November of 1837, Dr. Emerson was assigned to Louisiana, and there he met and married Eliza Irene Sanford. Now wanting his slaves, he sent for them, and they traveled on a steamboat down the Mississippi River to their master. They could have escaped in transit, but they did not. The stay in Louisiana was short, and the Emersons and the Scotts traveled back up the Mississippi on a steamboat to Fort Snelling. On the trip between the free state Illinois and the free Wisconsin Territory, Harriet gave birth to the Scotts' first daughter, Eliza, named after Mrs. Emerson.

In December of 1843, Dr. Emerson suddenly died at age 40, and his widow inherited his entire estate, including the Scotts. For the next three years, Mrs. Emerson rented the Scotts out, and eventually an army captain took Dred to the new state of Texas. In February 1846, Scott returned to St.

Louis, Missouri, and his family and he attempted to purchase his freedom from Mrs. Emerson. When she refused to support the transaction, Scott filed suit for the freedom of himself and his family, now consisting of a wife and two daughters.

REQUEST FOR FREEDOM

While it is not known why Scott did not request his freedom before, one theory is that Dr. Emerson may have promised to allow him to purchase his freedom if/when he was able to do so. Another theory is that the sons of Scott's previous owner, Peter Blow, informed him of his right to submit a legal claim for his freedom. Whatever the reason that eventually caused Scott to seek his freedom, a plethora of lawyers were willing to take the case. Based upon court decisions in similar cases in Missouri, it appeared to be a slam-dunk.

In *Winny v. Whitesides* (1824), the Missouri Supreme Court freed a slave who had been taken to the free state of Illinois. During the next 13 years, the same body was asked to rule on ten additional cases, and they declared all ten slaves free since they had either worked in a free jurisdiction or had lived there long enough to have been considered a resident. Similarly, courts in Kentucky, Louisiana, and Mississippi had also granted freedom to slaves who had lived for any significant length of time in a free state or territory. The precedent for emancipating a slave who resided in a free state or territory was established by *Somerset v. Stewart* (1772), a case in England. The British court said that the state of slavery is so "odious that nothing can be suffered to support it, but positive law.

COURT DECISION

In June of 1847, a Missouri circuit court ruled for Mrs. Emerson based on a technicality. While Scott was suing for his freedom from Mrs. Emerson, he could not produce a witness to testify to the fact that she owned him. A new trial was ordered in 1847 by the circuit court judge, but Mrs. Emerson's attorneys challenged this order before the Missouri Supreme Court. Delay followed delay, and the challenge was finally answered by the Missouri Supreme Court in June of 1848, indicating that Scott's trial could be heard again by the circuit court. The circuit court judge informed the jury that proof of Scott's residence in free jurisdictions would demolish his status as a slave. When the jury came to the conclusion that Scott had lived in free jurisdictions, the court declared him and his family to be free.

Since Mrs. Emerson did not want to lose her four slaves, she appealed the circuit court decision to the Missouri Supreme Court. In 1852, the Missouri Supreme Court reversed the lower court's decision. Scott–and his family– were still slaves. As expressed by Hamline University law professor Paul Finkelman, the decision was a political one, not one based on precedential law. The court's decision was based on "popular prejudice."

The Chief Justice of the Missouri Supreme Court was William Scott, and his decision overturned twenty-eight years of precedent-setting cases in the state. He wrote:
States have been possessed with a dark and fell spirit in relation to slavery, whose gratification is sought in the pursuit of measures, whose inevitable consequence must be the overthrow and destruction of our Government. Under such circumstances, it does not behoove the State of

Missouri to show the least countenance to any measure which might gratify this spirit.

FILED IN FEDERAL COURT

Once the Missouri Supreme Court ruled on Scott's suit, Mrs. Emerson probably assumed that the issue was settled. One of Scott's attorneys had died, and the other had left the state. Once acquired, his new attorneys began a new case–this time in federal court.

Scott's new attorney was Roswell Field, originally a New Englander with strong abolitionist opinions. Because of his beliefs, Field served Scott *pro bono*. Since Mrs. Emerson's brother-in-law John Sanford, a New York resident, had been acting on her behalf and was exerting control over the Scotts, the lawsuit was filed against him.

Field believed that the case filed in federal court was definitely winnable. Field filed the case in the United States Circuit Court, claiming battery and false imprisonment. Federal court was the route Field chose to take, claiming that the court had diversity jurisdiction with the claimant being from one state (Missouri) and the defendant being from another (New York).

The federal court system is composed of three levels:
- Federal District Court, which is basically the trial court.
- The Circuit Court, which is primarily a court of appeals.
- The United States Supreme Court.

Sanford's attorneys did not question that Scott was from Missouri and that their client was from New York.

Instead, they claimed that Scott, as a negro, was not a citizen and, therefore, the court had no jurisdiction in the matter. The court rejected Sanford's claim. Circuit court Judge Robert Wells, a slave owner originally from Virginia, did believe that blacks had "minimal legal rights, which included the right to sue in federal court." Article III of the United States Constitution granted a free, non-slave "citizen" rights. The question to be answered was whether Scott was free.

Thus, Sanford had to defend himself in court. In answer to the charges of battery and unlawful imprisonment, he responded that he had "gently" laid his hands on Scott and his family and that he had justifiably restrained them of their liberty since they were slaves. Upon completion of the arguments, Judge Wells instructed the jury that their decision was to be determined by the law of the state of Missouri. Since the Supreme Court of Missouri had already declared Scott to be a slave, the U.S. Circuit Court jury affirmed the decision that Scott was still a slave, and they found for Sanford.

APPEAL TO THE U.S. SUPREME COURT

An appeal to the United States Supreme Court followed the circuit court decision. Attorney Field was no longer involved, and an appeal to the Supreme Court was more expensive than the sons of former owner Blow could afford. Montgomery Blair, a Washington lawyer, agreed to take the case *pro bono*. Blair was not an abolitionist and could not have cared less about the Scotts and their freedom. What he was, however, was a member of the Free-Soil branch of the Democratic Party that opposed the spread of slavery into the territories. Sanford retained several attorneys to represent his interests, and the most prominent of his team was Reverdy Johnson, a Marylander who had the reputation of being one of the best Constitutional lawyers in the nation. He was also a very close friend of Roger Taney, Chief Justice of the Supreme Court.

The Justices that heard the Dred Scott case were geographically balanced. Five of the justices were from slave states in the South: James Wayne of Georgia, John Catron of Tennessee, Peter Daniel of Virginia, John Campbell of Alabama, and Taney of Maryland. All five came from slave–owning families; however, Taney and Wayne no longer owned any. The remaining four–John McLean of Ohio, Robert Grier of Pennsylvania, Samuel Nelson of New York, and Benjamin Curtis of Massachusetts–were northerners.

THE SUPREME COURT OF 1856

Expectation of a 5-4 vote based upon geography is deceptive. Only Daniel and Curtis had been appointed by northern Presidents. The other seven had been appointed by southern, slave-owning Presidents. In addition, eight of the nine Justices had been appointed by a Democratic President. Only Curtis had been appointed by Whig President Millard Fillmore. Two of the four northern justices–Nelson and Grier–were considered to be "doughfaces," the name given to northerners with southern sympathies. Soon-to-be-inaugurated President, James Buchanan was considered to be a "doughface."

Chief Justice Roger Taney was reared in a wealthy, Maryland family that made its fortune in land speculation, slave trading, and raising tobacco. According to historian Paul Finkelman: *Taney was a firm supporter of the right to own slaves and a staunch opponent to black rights. By the 1850s Taney was a seething, angry, uncompromising supporter of the south and slavery and an implacable foe of racial equality, the Republican Party, and the antislavery movement.*

Taney had served as Andrew Jackson's Attorney General, and, while in that office, had made several telling statements of his sentiments.

- The only rights blacks enjoy are those provided through the "sufferance and mercy of whites."
- Even when free, blacks were "a degraded class whose privileges were accorded to them as a matter of kindness and benevolence rather than right."

Thus, the Supreme Court that would hear and decide the Dred Scott case was not one likely to rule favorably to granting the slave's freedom. Most of the justices had decided before they heard any arguments, and, as stated by Finkelman, only "one justice, John McLean, openly opposed slavery."

CHOICES THE COURT HAD

The Supreme Court could have ruled on Scott's case by referring to *Strader v. Graham* (1851), a decision that stated the residence in a free state suspended slave status only temporarily. Under the *Strader* decision, the Court could have reaffirmed the stance that Scott's status turned on Missouri law, and Missouri law had determined that Scott and his family were still slaves. As put forward by historians Hofstadter, Miller, and Aaron, "The justices might simply have dismissed the case on the grounds that Scott was not a United States citizen and hence was not entitled to sue in federal court."

APPEAL TO THE U.S. SUPREME COURT

The Court knew, however, that the incoming Democratic President desired a showdown regarding the question of slavery in the territories. Hofstadter stated: *Buchanan had even gone so far as to indicate his desire to Justices Catron and Grier while the case was pending. Moreover, the justices seem to have concluded that so much public expectation and concern had been aroused that all the questions in the case should be discussed.*

BUCHANAN'S INVOLVEMENT

On the way to the podium to take his oath of office on Inauguration Day, Buchanan stopped briefly to speak with Chief Justice Taney. Many historians, along with William Seward of New York and Abraham Lincoln, believed that Taney, in that brief conversation, informed the incoming President what the decision would be. Historian Finkelman wrote that regardless of the conversation between Buchanan and Taney, the President-Elect knew in advance what the decision was going to be. "In a major breach of Court etiquette, Justice Robert C. Grier . . . had kept the president-elect fully informed about the progress of the case. . . ."

In his inaugural address on March 4, 1857, James Buchanan mentioned the Dred Scott decision that would be handed down two days later on March 6, 1857. Buchanan said that he would accept the forthcoming decision regarding Scott, and he urged the nation to do likewise. Finkelman continued, "There may not have been an ongoing conspiracy, but collusion abounded. The Court and the president-elect worked closely to get the decision

Buchanan and Taney wanted and to get the nation to accept it."

THE QUESTIONS TO BE ANSWERED

Chief Justice Taney wrote:
Can a negro, whose ancestors were imported into this country, and sold as slaves, become a member of the political community formed and brought into existence by the Constitution of the United States, and as such become entitled to all the rights, and privileges, and immunities, guarantied by that instrument to the citizen? One of which rights is the privilege of suing in a court of the United States in the cases specified in the Constitution.

The major debate going on within the nation at this time crystallized around three primary questions.

- Question Number 1: Could blacks sue in federal court as state citizens and as citizens of the United States?
- Question Number 2: Did Congress have the power to prohibit slavery in the territories? In other words, was the Missouri Compromise constitutional?
- Question Number 3: Was Missouri obligated to recognize Dred Scott's freedom based on his residence in either Illinois or the Wisconsin Territory?

THE MISSOURI COMPROMISE

With the purchase of the Louisiana Territory in 1803, the United States essentially doubled in size. As new states were admitted to the Union in the following years, the balance for political power was a major concern of both the

North and the South. The wrangling in Congress increased in intensity. In 1819, the situation reached its boiling point when Missouri was being considered for admission as a state. At that time, the Union was divided into 11 free states and 11 slaves states; however, Representative Tallmadge of New York introduced an amendment to the legislation admitting Missouri, prohibiting the introduction of any additional slaves. Furthermore, all children of current slaves in Missouri were to be freed when they reached the age of 25.

Through the efforts of Henry Clay, a compromise was reached when Maine sought admission to the Union. Maine would come in as a free state, and Missouri would join as a slave state, maintaining the balance of power in the Senate. The most significant provision stated that slavery would be prohibited "forever in all territory ceded by France to the United States . . . which lies north of 36°30'." The territory where slavery was forbidden included Illinois and the Wisconsin Territory, two of the states where Scott had resided as a slave while in the possession of Dr. Emerson.

THE COURT'S DECISION

Note, John F.A. Sanford spelled his last name with only one "d." The Supreme Court reporter spelled his last name Sandford. Therefore, the case is known as *Scott v. Sandford*. The U.S. Supreme Court handed down a 7-2 decision in the case of *Dred Scott v. Sandford*. Since both President-Elect Buchanan and Chief Justice Taney wanted the question of slavery in the territories settled once and for all, the decision went further than answering Dred Scott's petition.

RESPONSE TO QUESTION 1

Could blacks sue in federal court as state citizens and as citizens of the United States?

No.

Taney wrote:
[Blacks] *were not included, and were not intended to be included, under the word "citizens" in the Constitution, and can therefore claim none of the rights and privileges which that instrument provides for and secures to citizens of the United States.* Taney continued: *On the contrary, they were at that time [1787] considered as a subordinate and inferior class of beings, who had been subjugated by the dominant race, and, whether emancipated or not, yet remained subject to their authority, and had no rights or privileges but such as those who held the power and the Government might choose to grant them.* Taney concluded his opinion in regards to Scott's claim of citizenship by writing that blacks were *so far inferior that they had no rights which the white man was bound to respect.*

RESPONSE TO QUESTIONS 2 AND 3

Did Congress have the power to prohibit slavery in the territories? Was Missouri obligated to recognize Dred Scott's freedom based on his residence in either Illinois or the Wisconsin Territory?

No and No. In essence, the response to Question 1 answered both Questions 2 and 3.

The Missouri Compromise was unconstitutional. To answer these questions, Taney relied on his own interpretation of the Territories Clause and the Fifth Amendment to the Constitution.

Article IV, section 3, paragraph 2, of the Constitution reads: *The Congress shall have power to dispose of and make all needful rules and regulations respecting the territory or other property belonging to the United States. . . .* Taney interpreted this clause narrowly, saying that it referred only to the territory acquired in the treaty with England that ended the Revolutionary War. As posited by historian Paul Finkelman, Taney's "goal was to prohibit congressional regulation of slavery in the territories, and any argument, it seems, would do the trick."

Taney's use of the Fifth Amendment was his primary argument. In part, Amendment V states that no person shall be "deprived of life, liberty, or property, without the due process of law. . . ." Taney held that slaves were property, and the "right of property in a slave is distinctly and expressly affirmed in the Constitution." Since all states and territories abide under the protection of the United States Constitution, no state or territory could deny the right of a citizen to maintain possession of his property.

The Missouri Compromise was unconstitutional as would be any efforts by states to declare the right to decide whether it would be slave or free by popular sovereignty.

IN CONCLUSION

Thus in 1857, a little more than 50 years after *Marbury v. Madison*, the Supreme Court of the United States declared another act of Congress, the Missouri Compromise, to be unconstitutional.

RESULTS OF THE DECISION

Taney and Buchanan assumed that the Court's decision would end the debate on slavery, both in the Congress and in the states and territories. The decision, however, ultimately served as a major Republican issue in the 1858 elections and in the 1860 presidential election. While Lincoln and the other Republicans believed that the Dred Scott decision was a conspiracy to nationalize slavery, Lincoln maintained that it was the law of the land until the law was changed.

THE AFTERMATH

With the outbreak of the Civil War, any protection that slavery had experienced from the time of the creation of the United States Constitution ended. Slavery in the territories was ended by Lincoln's signing legislation to that effect on June 19, 1862. On January 1, 1863, Lincoln issued the Emancipation Proclamation.

In early 1865, Congress passed the Thirteenth Amendment, officially ending slavery and sent it on to the states for their approval.

On July 28, 1868, the Fourteenth Amendment was ratified, granting citizenship to "all persons born or naturalized in the United States."

On March 30, 1870, the Fifteenth Amendment was ratified, guaranteeing all male citizens of the United States the right to vote.

DRED SCOTT

Unfortunately, Dred Scott did not live long enough to see the Supreme Court decision negated. Shortly after the Taney Court handed down its decision, the Blow Brothers, the sons of Scott's original owner Peter Blow, purchased the Scott family and granted them their freedom. According to Historian Finkelman, "Dred Scott remained a free man, and something of a celebrity, from May 26, 1857, until his death from tuberculosis nine months later, on February 17, 1858."

PLESSY V. FERGUSON (1896)

Louisiana enacted the Separate Car Act that required separate railway cars for blacks and whites. Homer Plessy–who was seven-eighths Caucasian–agreed to participate in a test to challenge the Act. The Supreme Court held segregation did not in itself constitute unlawful discrimination.

~ OYEZ

INTRODUCTION

Prior to the Civil War, slaves were considered chattel (property) of their owners and could be treated or disposed of in whatever way the master desired. The treatment of slaves in the South was loosely based on the *Code Noir*, a decree issued by Louis XIV in 1685 that defined the conditions of slavery in the French colonies. Provisions of the *Code Noir* set rules for slaves and slave owners regarding religion, sexual relations and marriage, punishments, prohibitions, and freedom. Treatment of the slaves in the antebellum South was loosely based on the *Code Noir.*

Passage of the Thirteenth Amendment in 1865 provided:
Neither slavery nor involuntary servitude, except as a punishment for crime whereof the party shall have been duly convicted, shall exist with the United States, or any place subject to their jurisdiction.

POST-CIVIL WAR

Following the Civil War, the Reconstruction Acts of 1867-68 divided the South into five military districts, and federal troops were assigned to the South to make sure that the vanquished states abided by the tenets of the Acts. To be readmitted to the Union, each of the southern states had to ratify the Fourteenth Amendment to the United States Constitution.

Section 1 of the Amendment states in part:
All persons born or naturalized in the United States, and subject to the jurisdiction thereof, are citizens of the United States and of the State wherein they reside.

In response to the Thirteenth and Fourteenth amendments, most southern states' legislatures passed laws referred to as the Black Codes. The purpose of the Codes was primarily to assure that White Supremacy continued within the South by the Black Codes restricting former slaves access to restaurants, taverns, and soda shops. Protests and boycotts by African Americans had some significant results in Louisiana and some of the other states, and one by one old traditions and practices began to give way to new laws requiring equal rights for all citizens regardless of color.

In 1868, Louisiana's "Black and Tan" Constitution was adopted, outlawing racial segregation in public places and public accommodations. The conservative press of Louisiana vigorously criticized the new document. One paper wrote that the Constitution committed "crimes against reason, against religion, and against nature." Another called the Constitution "a condensed charter of all the turpitudes and monstrosities which Negro depravity and fanatical partisanship are attempting to impose upon us."

FIFTEENTH AMENDMENT

The Fifteenth Amendment to the United States Constitution was ratified on March 30, 1870. Section 1 stated in part: *The right of citizens of the United States to vote shall not be denied or abridged by the United States or by State on account of race, color, or previous condition of servitude.*

THE CIVIL RIGHTS ACT OF 1875

The Civil Rights Act of 1875 was the last major Reconstruction statute, and it guaranteed African Americans equal treatment in public transportation and in public accommodations. In March 1883, the United States Supreme Court ruled that the Act was unconstitutional, robbing both the Thirteenth and Fourteenth amendments of much of their meaning. This ruling remained in force until the Court upheld the Civil Rights Act of 1964, nearly 100 years later.

COMPROMISE OF 1877

As long as federal troops were present in the South, rights that blacks had gained from the Thirteenth, Fourteenth, and Fifteenth amendments remained in place. The election of 1876, however, changed everything. The Republican candidate was Rutherford B. Hayes, and his Democratic opponent was Samuel J. Tilden. Louisiana, Florida, and South Carolina were still under "Republican carpetbagger" control, and these states went to Hayes. In order to gain the electoral votes from the three southern states, a non-written agreement was negotiated, pledging that federal troops would be withdrawn from the South, in essence, issuing the formal end of Reconstruction. Although Tilden won the popular vote, Hayes won the presidency with an electoral vote of 185-184.

THE AGE OF JIM CROW

With the absence of federal troops, the southern states returned to conducting their affairs as they saw fit, and a tide of racism began to mount unopposed. According to historian C. Vann Woodward: *"Jim Crow" as a symbol originated with a minstrel, "Daddy" Rice, who in 1832 introduced a blackface act ('Weel a-bout and turn a-bout/And . . . Jump Jim Crow') based on the antics of a slave of that name.*

The social reality of Jim Crow laws began much later with a bill supporting the segregating of passengers on a train. The bill entitled "An Act To Promote the Comfort of Passengers" was passed by the Louisiana legislature on July 10, 1890. When the bill was initially introduced in he legislature, the American Citizens' Equal Rights Association of Louisiana filed a petition opposing it. This organization of colored people claimed that the idea was "unconstitutional, un-American, unjust, dangerous and against sound public policy." The new law required railroads "to provide equal but separate accommodations for the white and the colored races." Opponents of the new law blamed the sixteen African American members of the Assembly for its passage, saying that the sixteen legislators could have killed the proposal early on.

Waxing even more philosophical, the Equal Rights Association declared that the law would "be a free license to the evilly-disposed that they might with impunity insult, humiliate, and otherwise maltreat inoffensive persons, and especially women and children who should happen to have dark skin."

BLACK COMMUNITY RESPONSE

L.A. Martinet, the editor of a newspaper advocating black rights and privileges named *Crusader,* and R.L. Desdunes, both members of the Equal Rights Association, designed a plan. Eighteen men were formed into the Citizens' Committee to Test the constitutionality of the Separate Car Law.

Martinet was a forty-four-year-old newspaper editor who combined his editorializing and writing with social activism. Of mixed races, Martinet was viewed as a hero by many for fighting against segregation from within the deep South. The needed funds to launch the venture were raised from donations, and Albion Winegar Tourgée, a lawyer from New York, was appointed lead attorney in the case. Tourgée and Martinet worked together and developed a mutual admiration relationship.

Tourgée was a fifty-four-year-old lawyer/novelist whom historian Woodward called "the most famous surviving carpetbagger [in 1890]" primarily because of the six novels that he had written about his Reconstruction experiences in North Carolina. He was born in Ohio of French Huguenot descent and fought in the Union Army. Once he had arrived in North Carolina in 1865, he soon became a leader of the Radical Republican Party. According to historian Woodward, Tourgée "took a prominent part in writing of the Radical Constitution of North Carolina, and served as a judge of the superior court for six years with considerable distinction."

THE PLAN

The initial plan to attack the new law was developed by Tourgée, Martinet, and James C. Walker, a local attorney. The plan called for sending a "nearly white" male to buy a first-class ticket, enter the first-class car, and then be confronted by a previously informed conductor who would attempt to remove the man. When the "nearly white" subject refused to leave, he would be arrested. Then, the team of crusaders could swing into action.

The first person selected was a young man of light color named Daniel F. Desdunes. On February 24, 1892, he purchased a first-class ticket and boarded a train in Mobile, Alabama. Everything worked perfectly, except the court then declared that the law prohibiting blacks from riding in the first-class white car was only for intrastate travel and did not apply to interstate passengers. Desdunes was an interstate passenger holding a ticket to Alabama. The case was dismissed.

THE NEW PLAN

On June 1, 1892, Martinet wired Tourgée that Walker had suggested that they try another test case, this time wholly within a state. On June 1, Homer Adolph Plessy bought a first-class ticket on the East Louisiana Railroad that was scheduled to take him from New Orleans to Covington, Louisiana.

Born on March 17, 1862, in New Orleans, Louisiana, Homère Patrice Adolphe Plessy lost his father when he was young. His mother remarried a post office clerk who was from a family of shoemakers, a trade that Plessy learned and practiced as an adult. Plessy's stepfather was also a social activist, and his stepson followed in those footsteps, joining a group called the Protective Educational and Social Club. The organization's primary goal was in seeking educational equality for children of color. Plessy was a member of *the gens de couleur,* the class consisting of free Creole people of color in Louisiana. He was reportedly one-eighth colored and seven-eighths white, having had one grandparent who was a person of color.

During both the former attempt with Desdunes and the Plessy event, it was apparent that the railroad knew of the plan and had agreed to participate. Since playing the enforcer of this law was not what the railroad companies wanted to do, their assistance in the effort to have it declared illegal was not surprising.

Once seated in the train's first-class car, Plessy announced to J.J. Dowling, the conductor, "I have to tell you that, according to Louisiana law, I am a colored man." When he refused the conductor's instruction to retire to the "colored car," Chris Cain, a private detective on the car, arrested Plessy. Cain accompanied Plessy to the New Orleans police station on Elysian Fields Avenue where he was booked. The punishment was a twenty-five dollar fine or twenty days in jail. The treasurer of the Citizens' Committee provided the $500 bail for Plessy, offering his house as security.

The two attorneys, Tourgée and Walker, were hoping that the local court would find Plessy guilty. A guilty decision would allow them to appeal the case, and they hoped to appeal it the entire way to the U. S. Supreme Court. The *Times-Democrat* of New Orleans reported: "It is generally believed that Plessy intends testing the law before the courts."

IN THE LOUISIANA COURTS

The judge of Section A of the Criminal District Court for the Parish of Louisiana was John H. Ferguson. When Plessy's attorneys, Tourgée and Walker, pled that the Jim Crow law was null and void because of its being unconstitutional, Ferguson overruled. At this point, the case became known as *Plessy v. Ferguson*. Tourgée then appealed the case to the Louisiana Supreme Court, and a hearing was held in November of 1892. The only question, said the court, was whether the Jim Crow Law violated the Fourteenth Amendment.

On December 19, 1892, Justice Charles E. Fenner handed down the decision, ruling that neither the Thirteenth Amendment nor the Fourteenth Amendment was violated by the Jim Crow Car Law. Citing two lower court decisions, he ruled that segregation was not discriminatory since it applied to both races. One of the cases that Justice Fenner cited was *West Chester and Philadelphia Railroad Company v. Miles* (1867). In that case, segregation was justified by Justice Daniel Agnew who wrote that God had created the races dissimilar so that they did not "overstep the cultural boundaries He had assigned to them."

THE UNITED STATES SUPREME COURT

Following the Louisiana Supreme Court decision, racial tensions in the South rose. The Ku Klux Klan's activity intensified, and a major economic depression caused by the Panic of 1893 was underway. Tourgée recommended that the appeal to the U.S. Supreme Court be delayed a little, hoping for more favorable times. Unfortunately for Plessy and his legal counsel, the time did not become more favorable. In fact, the nation, in general, had become more supportive of segregation, and the Court, in specific, had become more conservative. As posited by historian Woodward, in the time between the passage of the Louisiana segregation law in 1890 and the eventual hearing before the Supreme Court six years later, national attitudes had changed. "The retreat from the commitment to equality had quickened its pace in the South and met with additional acquiescence, encouragement, and approval in the North."

A conservative Court existed in 1896 comprised of Justices George Shiras, Jr.; Rufus Wheeler Peckham; Stephen Johnson Field; Horace Gray; Henry Billings Brown; John Marshall Harlan; David Josiah Brewer; Edward Douglass White; and Chief Justice Melville W. Fuller–six Republicans and three Democrats.

- Stephen Johnson Field, although a Democrat from Connecticut, was nominated by Abraham Lincoln. Hesitant about using the Fourteenth Amendment to protect the rights of African Americans, Field had previously dissented on two cases that upheld the right of blacks to serve on juries.
- Horace Gray, born into a wealthy Massachusetts family, was nominated by Chester Arthur, a Republican President. Although a member of the Free-Soil Party and a critic of Roger Taney's Dred Scott opinion, he would not go against the Court's interpretation of the Thirteenth and Fourteenth amendments.
- Melville Weston Fuller, a Democrat nominated by Grover Cleveland, became Chief Justice and was a supporter of Stephen Douglas in his race against Lincoln. Not a strong advocate for the North during the Civil War, he supported a state constitutional amendment that denied blacks the right to vote. He had previously denounced the Emancipation Proclamation.

- David Josiah Brewer was a Republican nominated by Benjamin Harrison. He was a strong proponent of the Tenth Amendment and an advocate for keeping the states free of federal government interference.
- George Shiras, Jr., a Republican from Pennsylvania, had been nominated by Benjamin Harrison. Not considered to have had an independent mind, Shiras tended to side with the majority.
- Edward Douglas White, nominated by Democrat Grover Cleveland, was a Roman Catholic, southern gentleman from Louisiana. According to an unverified report, at one time White was associated with the Ku Klux Klan. White fought for the Confederacy during the Civil War.
- Rufus Wheeler Peckham, nominated by Democrat Grover Cleveland, was from a prominent New York family. At the time of *Plessy v. Ferguson*, Peckham was the newest member of the Court .
- Chief Justice Melville Fuller was a conservative Democrat from Illinois. Fuller had initiated the "conference handshake" practice that still continues in the Court. Upon completion of deliberation, the Justices shake hands to remind them, as historian Joan Axelrod-Contrada wrote, "Though their opinions may differ, they share a common purpose."

BLACK COMMUNITY LACK OF RESPONSE

The lack of support by two significant black leaders did not help the Plessy cause. Abolitionist and former slave Frederick Douglass chose not to support the case, believing that the case would be lost and would hurt the cause of racial equality.

The other black leader who did not lend support to Plessy's situation was Booker T. Washington. In 1895, Washington delivered a speech that has been called the Atlanta Compromise Address. In essence, he told blacks to stop working so hard for social and political equality. Instead, he encouraged them to lift themselves up economically and prove themselves worthy of the respect of whites.

PLESSY'S ARGUMENT

Some of Tourgée's arguments attempted to appeal to the Court's conservatism, and he developed multiple points to deliver at the hearing. His primary arguments were that requiring blacks to ride in a segregated railroad car was a violation of both the Thirteenth and the Fourteenth amendments.

FERGUSON'S ARGUMENT

Alexander Morse, representing Ferguson and the state of Louisiana, argued that the law was reasonable because it applied to both whites and blacks and was, therefore, non-discriminatory. He further argued that the responsibility to enforce the Fourteenth Amendment was the state's under police powers, a concept presented by the Court in the *Civil Rights Cases* of 1883.

THE COURT'S DECISION

The question that the Court had to answer: Does the Louisiana statue providing "equal but separate railway carriages for the whites and colored violate the Thirteenth and Fourteenth amendments?"

The Answer: No!

Justice Henry Brown delivered the majority opinion reflecting a 7 to 1 vote, making the following points:

- The Louisiana law requiring blacks to ride in a segregated (Jim Crow) car is not a violation of the Thirteenth Amendment. The Court's response on this point was labeled by Brown as "too clear to argue."
- "In the nature of things, the Fourteenth Amendment of the Constitution was only concerned about legal, not social, equality." Brown went on to opine that the Amendment "could not have been intended to abolish distinctions based upon color, or to enforce social, as distinguished from political, equality.
- Brown also denied that segregation of the races by law "stamps the colored race with a badge of inferiority," as claimed by Plessy's counsel, or "a commingling of the two races upon terms unsatisfactory to either."
- Outlawing segregation would not eliminate racial prejudice because such societal attitudes would not be changed by simply changing the law.
- Since the Louisiana law did not conflict with the Fourteenth Amendment, the only remaining question was whether the law was "reasonable and . . . enacted in good faith the promotion for the public good."

Since the Court believed that it furthered "the preservation of the public peace and good order, . . ." the law met this requirement.

IN CONCLUSION

Thus, in 1896, the Supreme Court of the United States declared:

- **The Louisiana law requiring blacks to ride in a segregated (Jim Crow) car was not a violation of the Thirteenth Amendment.**
- **" . . . The Fourteenth Amendment of the Constitution was only concerned about legal, not social, equality."**
- **"If one race be inferior to the other socially, the Constitution . . . cannot put them upon the same plane."**

A DISSENTING OPINION

The lone dissenting opinion was offered by Justice John Marshall Harlan. He was born in Kentucky in 1833, the son of a lawyer who named him after the famous Supreme Court Chief Justice. The Harlan Family owned slaves but "treated them with paternalistic good will."

Originally a Democrat, Harlan switched to the Republican Party following the Civil War for an unknown reason. On his desk, Harlan maintained the inkwell used by former Chief Justice Taney, primary author of the Dred Scott decision, a reminder of "the shame in denying blacks the right of citizenship," according to historian Axelrod-Contrada.

Justice John Marshall Harlan submitted the lone dissenting opinion, positing the following:
- Segregationist legislation, like the Louisiana law, was based on the assumption that "colored citizens are so inferior and degraded that they cannot be

allowed to sit in public coaches occupied by white citizens."

- Judge Harlan opined that the outcome of the Louisiana law continued the fallacious belief that African Americans were inferior to whites. By allowing the Louisiana law to remain in effect, Harlan believed that the government was permitting "the seed of race hate to be planted under the sanction of the law."
- The Constitution must be "color-blind," and it could allow "no superior, dominant ruling class of citizens."
- Harlan argued if the state may so regulate the railroads, "Why may it not so regulate the use of the streets of its cities and towns as to compel white citizens to keep on one side of a street, and black citizens to keep on the other?"
- Harlan concluded his dissent by presciently writing: "In my opinion, the judgment this day rendered will, in time prove to be quite as pernicious as the decision made by this tribunal in the Dred Scott Case."

Harlan believed that since the Louisiana law in effect created classes, it was unconstitutional.

THE AFTERMATH

The "separate but equal" verdict of the highest court in the land enabled and encouraged the Jim Crow laws to expand. In addition to separate train cars, schools, stores, restrooms, water fountains, restaurants, churches, laundries, entrances to theaters, seating in theaters, housing, hospitals, bars, cemeteries, and many other laws and practices followed. The *Richmond Times*, agreeing with the Supreme Court endorsed view of the relationship between blacks and whites read: *It is necessary that this principle be applied in every relation of Southern life. God Almighty drew the color line and it cannot be obliterated. The negro must stay on his side of the line and the white man must stay on his side, and the sooner both races recognize this fact and accept it, the better it will be for both.*

Newspaper coverage of *Plessy v. Ferguson* in the North was sparse. The *New York Times* included a small article on a page with railroad news. The *Republican* of Springfield, Massachusetts, compared Jim Crow to a disease, predicting, "The law may be expected to spread like the measles in those commonwealths where white supremacy is thought to be in peril."

Soon after the verdict was rendered, Martinet suspended his publication of the *Crusader,* and the Citizen Committee made one more public statement before disbanding.
Notwithstanding the [Supreme Court] decision . . . we, as freemen, still believe that we were right and our cause is sacred. We are encouraged by the indomitable will and noble defense of Hon. Albion W. Tourgée, and supported by the courageous dissenting opinion of Justice John Harlan in behalf of justice and equal rights. In defending the cause of liberty, we met with defeat, but not with ignominy.

With the decision by the Supreme Court, Homer Plessy returned to Section A of the criminal court to face the charges against him. Changing his plea from not guilty to guilty, he was given a choice of a fine of $25 or twenty days in prison. He paid the fine. Homer Plessy lived the remainder of his years in relative obscurity, working in a variety of jobs. Plessy's attorneys Walker and Tourgée died in 1898 and 1905, respectively. Judge Ferguson died in 1915. The publisher and advocate L.A. Martinet died on the twenty-fifth anniversary of Plessy's train ride.

Historian Axelrod-Contrada reported that when Plessy died, his "obituary was as unassuming as the man: 'Plessy–on Sunday, March 1, 1925, at 5:10 a.m. beloved husband of Louise Bordenave.'"

As written by historian Woodward: "*Plessy v. Ferguson* remained the law of the land for fifty-eight years lacking one day, from May 18, 1896, to May 17, 1954, when the Supreme Court at last renounced it in the school segregation cases of *Brown et al. v. Board of Education of Topeka, et al.*"

But that is a case for another day!

BROWN V. BOARD OF EDUCATION (1954)

The consolidation of four cases in which African American minors were denied entrance into certain public schools was reviewed by the Supreme Court.

The question the Court had to answer was "Does the segregation of public education based solely on race violate the equal Protection Clause of the Fourteenth Amendment?"

The unanimous decision was, "Yes."

~ OYEZ

INTRODUCTION

The Supreme Court's decision on *Dred Scott* in 1857 stood as the law of the land for less than a decade. The chronology that negated that decision:

- The Emancipation Proclamation, January 1, 1863
- Passage of the Thirteenth Amendment, February 1, 1865
- Passage of the Fourteenth Amendment, June 16, 1866
- Passage of the Fifteenth Amendment, February 27, 1869.

Reconstruction and the presence of federal troops throughout the South somewhat shielded the newly freed citizens from suffering immediate repercussions from white supremacists. With the removal of the troops in 1877 and the rise of the Ku Klux Klan, the lives of blacks were placed in jeopardy.

In response to the Emancipation Proclamation and the Thirteenth and Fourteenth amendments, "Black Codes" were developed and adopted in all southern states except Tennessee. Based primarily on the rights of free blacks prior to the war, African Americans were granted the right to sue, testify in court, marry, and attend school. They could not, however, vote, hold office, serve on a jury, bear arms, work as artisans, mechanics, or any position where they competed with whites for the job. Several Supreme Court civil rights decisions ruled that the federal government had no jurisdiction over matters of social discrimination directed by private individuals or organizations against persons of color. These decisions opened the door for the Jim Crow laws to be introduced.

JIM CROW LAWS

Beginning with the introduction of separate train cars for whites and blacks (*Plessy v. Ferguson*, 1896), the Jim Crow laws eventually expanded to include numerous "separate but equal" facilities and accommodations in southern life. While the "separate" part of the *Plessy* decision created two distinct societies, the "equal" part was seldom ever provided. Hotels, theaters, public lavatories, hospitals, schools, cemeteries, waiting rooms, etc., provided for blacks were generally inferior to those provided for whites.

Following the decision in *Plessy v. Ferguson*, the Jim Crow mantra of separate but equal remained the law of the land for more than half a century. To rid the land of these practices took the concerted efforts of individuals and organizations.

EARLY EFFORTS

One person of color who spoke out against racial discrimination was Booker T. Washington. His approach, however, did not challenge the Jim Crow laws. Instead, he encouraged the black citizen to work for economic independence and to gain equality through that means.

THE RISE OF THE NAACP

Another civil rights advocate of the early twentieth century was W.E.B. Du Bois. Starting with the Niagara Movement in 1905, Du Bois, a graduate of Harvard University, joined with white proponents of racial equality and spoke out for equal treatment. On February 12, 1909, the one-hundredth anniversary of Abraham Lincoln's birth, a significant number of civil rights activists joined with Du Bois and the Niagara Movement to form the National Association for the Advancement of Colored People (NAACP). Du Bois became the editor of the NAACP's publication, *Crisis*. The purpose of *Crisis* was to share the political, social, and educational struggles the blacks were experiencing in a nation that was founded on the principle that all "men are created equal."

Born in Barrington, Massachusetts, William Edward Burghardt (W.E.B.) Du Bois was a sociologist, writer, and activist who taught at Wilberforce University and Atlanta University. He "published 19 books, edited four magazines, coedited a magazine for children, and produced scores of articles and speeches." In 1948, disputes within the NAACP caused Du Bois to be dismissed, and he eventually joined the American Communist Party. Under the leadership of Du Bois, the NAACP initiated numerous lawsuits to publicize racial injustices. Du Bois, James

Weldon Johnson, Walter White, Thurgood Marshall, and others attempted to secure equal education, employment, housing, and public accommodations for African Americans.

James Weldon Johnson was a songwriter, poet, novelist, journalist, critic, lawyer, and biographer. Serving as the field secretary of the NAACP, he edited numerous books recording the words to Negro spirituals. Johnson wrote polemic treatises refuting biased commentary by white critics.

Walter Francis White served as the executive secretary of the NAACP from 1931 to 1955. He is considered to be one of the major architects of the modern African American struggle for freedom. Born with blond hair and blue eyes, White used his "white" features to infiltrate the Ku Klux Klan and other white supremacist organizations.

THURGOOD MARSHALL

While Johnson and White accomplished significant inroads in the fight to end segregation, the person most associated with the eventual end to "separate but equal" was Thurgood Marshall, the grandson of slaves. Born on July 2, 1908, Marshall's original name given by his parents was Thoroughgood. Eventually, Marshall unilaterally shortened his name to Thurgood. The son of a railroad porter and an elementary teacher, Marshall graduated with honors from Lincoln University after being rejected by the University of Maryland because he was not white. After graduation from Howard Law School, Marshall practiced law in Baltimore. His first major victory was *Murray v. Pearson* (1935) in which he successfully sued the University of Maryland for denying entrance to a student based solely on race.

In 1936, Marshall was hired as a staff lawyer for the NAACP, and by 1940 he had become the chief of the organization's Legal Defense and Educational Fund, a post that he held until 1961. In his role as chief counsel in the 1940's, Marshall chipped away at Jim Crow and the solid wall of segregation in the South. According to historian James T. Patterson, "The three most powerful forces behind change in American race relations at the time [were] . . ." rising militancy among blacks, vocal support from liberals like Gunnar Myrdal and President Harry Truman, and the activism of Thurgood Marshall.

MARSHALL IN THE SUPREME COURT

During the 1940s and 1950s, Marshall built a reputation as one of the top lawyers in the country, arguing before the United States Supreme Court on 32 cases. He won 29 of those 32 cases! Two examples of cases Marshall argued and won before the Supreme Court are *Chambers v. Florida* and *Smith v. Allwright*. Marshall's first case for the U.S. Supreme Court was *Chambers v. Florida*, in which he defended four black men who had been convicted of murdering a white man. The conviction was based upon their confessions that had been given under coercion. The Court voted unanimously to overturn their conviction.

In *Smith v. Allwright* (1944), Democrats in Texas and several other southern states had initiated what they called a "whites-only primary." The Court ruled that the respective Democratic parties were not "private organizations," and blacks could not be denied the right to vote.

A CHANGE OF FOCUS

During the late 1930s and early 1940s, Marshall and the NAACP focused on racist practices that were occurring in publicly supported graduate and professional schools. At the beginning, they did not challenge the "separate" part of "separate but equal" ruling of *Plessy v. Ferguson*. Instead, they challenged the "equal" part.

In 1938, Lloyd Gaines, a graduate of Missouri's state-supported black college, was denied admission to the University of Missouri's Law School solely on the basis of his race. In December of 1938, the Supreme Court decided six to two in Gaines' favor. In 1939, Lloyd Gaines disappeared, never to be heard from again.

Twelve years later, Heman Sweatt, a negro mail carrier, was denied acceptance into the University of Texas Law School based on his race. Instead, Texas established an inadequate law school for blacks in the basement of one of their buildings. In 1950, after Marshall argued Sweatt's case to the Supreme Court, the Court declared that it could "not find substantial equality" in facilities and told UT to admit him.

On the same day as the Court handed down the decision on Sweatt, it also ruled on the appeal of George McLaurin, a sixty-eight-year-old teacher who applied for admission to the University of Oklahoma's educational doctorate program. Reluctantly admitted in 1949, McLaurin had to sit in an anteroom off the regular classroom, eat his meals in an alcove, and sit at a segregated desk in the mezzanine of the library when studying. The Court agreed and found for McLaurin.

Shortly after the *Sweatt* and *McLaurin* decisions, Marshall and the NAACP changed their focus. After consulting with state branch presidents in 1950, Marshall decided to end the search for equality and to attack the entire concept of segregation. Many of those who had the courage to join with Marshall and the NAACP to bring suit for equal treatment found themselves losing jobs, being intimidated, having their homes burned, being denied credit in stores, and unable to qualify for bank loans.

HEADING TO THE SUPREME COURT

In 1951, Linda Brown was a third grade student at Monroe School, a school for negro children in Topeka, Kansas. She wanted to attend summer school. To get to school, Linda had to leave home by 7:40 in the morning, walk six blocks through a railroad switching yard, cross Topeka's busiest commercial street, and board a bus to go to a school that began at 9:00 a.m. If segregation would not have been in effect, Linda could have attended a summer school program seven blocks from her home.

Oliver Brown, Linda's father, was a welder for the railroad and was an assistant pastor in the Methodist church that the Brown Family attended. He could not be considered a radical. Representing Brown and twelve other plaintiffs, Thurgood Marshall and the NAACP filed a suit in federal district court on February 28, 1951. Marshall, Jack Greenberg, and Robert Carter led the team in preparation for the eventual hearing in district court. Greenberg, a graduate of Columbia University, was a young, white attorney who would eventually succeed Marshall as head of the NAACP's Legal Defense and Educational Fund. Carter, a graduate of Lincoln University and Howard Law School, was a veteran of a segregated military unit during WWII and the most militant of the attorneys that worked with Marshall.

The strategy that they developed was unique. The team was not concerned about the travel time that Linda and the other children experienced or even the safety factor. The team did not complain that there were racially separate schools. (Though separate, the schools were basically equal.) Rather, as pointed out by Patterson:

What was intolerable . . . was that the system of segregation in Topeka was legally required, and that it was enforced. Children who were part of such an officially sanctioned system, they said, were made to feel inferior. And children who felt inferior would necessarily lose motivation to learn.

When the case was presented in federal district court, Judge Walter Huxman, speaking for a unanimous three-judge panel, found there was no violation of *Plessy v. Ferguson*. Although separate, the facilities were equal, and that was all that mattered. Segregation would continue in Topeka until a higher court overruled the decision. The federal district court, however, did attach nine findings of facts to its opinion. One of the nine stated: *Segregation of white and colored children in public schools has a detrimental effect upon the colored children. The impact is greater when it has the sanction of the law; for the policy of separating races is usually interpreted as demoting the inferiority of the Negro group. A sense of inferiority affects the motivation of a child to learn.*

THE UNITED STATES SUPREME COURT

During 1950 and 1951, the NAACP had represented each of the four other plaintiffs, each a losing cause in federal district courts. Each time, the respective courts upheld the *Plessy v. Ferguson* separate but equal decision. When Marshall filed an appeal with the United States Supreme Court, the Justices had to decide if they would hear the case or let the decision from the lower court stand. Ultimately, the Court decided not only to hear *Brown v. Board of Education*, but also to combine a total of five similar cases. The four other cases: *Briggs v. Elliott, Davis v. Board of Education, Gebhart v. Belton, Bolling v. Sharpe.*

BRIGGS V. ELLIOTT

Briggs v. Elliott was filed in Clarendon County, South Carolina, where the comparison of the equal part of separate but equal revealed great discrepancies.

According to historian James Patterson, in 1949-50, Clarendon County:
- Spent $149 per white child and $43 per black child.
- Built white schools of brick or stucco and had shanties for more than half of the black schools.
- Had average class size of 28 in the white schools and average class size of 47 in the black schools.
- Let one of the two black elementary schools have no running water and the other have no electricity.
- Let the white schools have flush toilets and the black schools have outhouses.
- Let the white schools have water fountains and the black schools have dippers in open buckets.
- Let white students be transported to school in buses and let black students walk.

Marshall found these conditions to be similar throughout the South.

DAVIS V. BOARD OF EDUCATION

Davis v. Board of Education of Prince Edward County was filed in Virginia. Robert R. Moton High School was a severely overcrowded black school in Farmville, Virginia. Curricular programs in that school were nowhere near the quality of the white high school. In addition, the highest paid teacher at Moton received less than the lowest paid teacher at the white high school.

GEBHART V. BELTON

Gebhart v. Belton was filed in Delaware, a border state. Black students were prohibited from attending an attractive, modern high school in Claymont, Delaware, but instead were bused to the old school that the new one had replaced. In the rural area outside of Claymont, white children were bused to elementary schools, but blacks were not.

BOLLING V. SHARPE

Bolling v. Sharpe was a case filed in Washington, D.C. "White flight" resulted in white schools in the city having excess room and black schools being crowded. The NAACP brought suit representing Spotswood Bolling who was not permitted to attend a white school that had space. Instead, the twelve-year-old had to attend a dingy, overcrowded black school.

The Supreme Court Justices that heard the cases in the spring of 1953 were Chief Justice Fred Vinson, Associate Justices Felix Frankfurter, Hugo Black, Stanley Reed, William Douglas, Tom Clark, Robert Jackson, Harold

Burton, and Sherman Minton. Following the hearing of the cases in the spring of 1953, the Court asked to rehear the cases in the fall of the same year. Not all of the Justices were initially of the same mind, and those favoring desegregation reportedly spent time trying to convince those who were not. From their conference notes and draft decisions, the Justices apparently did not all initially see the same response. Justices Douglas, Black, Burton, and Minton wanted to overturn the *Plessy* decision.

Justice Stanley Reed believed that the Court had to be cautious about states rights and initially indicated that he felt that segregation worked to the benefit of the African American community. Similarly, Justice Tom Clark, a Texan who had been Truman's attorney general, wrote that the Court had led the states to believe that segregation is acceptable, and they should be allowed to work it out. Justices Robert Jackson and Felix Frankfurter did not like segregation, but they were also opposed to judicial activism and were concerned about the enforceability of any prohibition on segregation.

Justice Fred Vinson was concerned that Congress had issued no legislation that addressed the need for desegregation; therefore, he seemed hesitant to strike down segregation. Vinson was a friend of Truman, but he was intellectually outshone by Black, Douglas, Frankfurter, and Jackson.

The Court that was to decide the issue of segregation was deeply divided in personality, experience, and style. While different philosophical existed opinions among the Justices, personal animosities amplified these differences. Vinson's serious, slow-moving style could not bring the Court together.

In September of 1953, Justice Vinson died. President Eisenhower appointed Earl Warren as Chief Justice, and the Senate confirmed his appointment. Prior to his appointment, Warren had supported the integration of Mexican Americans into California school systems.

CRAFTING THE DECISION

Warren's goal was generally to bring the Court together, working to overcome the animosities that were present. When the second hearing of *Brown et al.* concluded on December 9, though not all on the same page with a decision, the members agreed to keep discussing the topic, which they did for the next three months. By March, Warren had worked his magic in bringing the members of the Court to respect each other's opinions better, if not style. He wrote the first draft of his opinion that all eight of the Associate Justices could accept. A Texan, Associate Justice Reed was the last to give in after Warren reminded him that his dissent would encourage the South to resist the decision. Concurring with Warren's prediction, Reed capitulated.

THE DECISION

The Court was convened on May 17, 1954, and Chief Justice Earl Warren read the unanimous decision to the public. From the beginning of the Court's deliberation, the Chief Justice had said that the decision must be brief and clearly understandable. It was eleven pages long. Associate Justice Robert Jackson had suffered a serious heart attack several weeks before the decision was made public, and he had remained in the hospital until the day the decision was read. He chose to leave the hospital and be present for the announcement.

As Warren read more than halfway through the decision, citing past cases about segregation, he gave no indication which way the Court was ruling. Suspense was building. Then he read: **"Does segregation of children in public schools solely on the basis of race . . . deprive the children of the minority group of equal educational opportunities?"**

"We believe that it does."

To separate them [black children in grade and high schools] from others of similar age and qualifications solely because of their race generates a feeling of inferiority as to their status in the community that may affect their hearts and minds in a way unlikely ever to be undone. The decision said, bottom line, that *de jure* segregation in the United States of America is unconstitutional. *Plessy v. Ferguson* had been abolished. We conclude that in the field of education, the doctrine of "separate but equal" has no place.

The decision in *Brown v. Board of Education et al.* was not the end. It was only the end of the beginning. Southern whites fought back against the Court's decision, and leaders like Strom Thurmond and George Wallace rode the topic to fame.

THE AFTERMATH

As told by Hudgins and Vacca: "When the Court handed down the Brown decision, it asked for reargument on the question of how best to implement it." Realizing difficulty in dismantling a dual system that had been in place for decades, the Court would meet again in 1955 in what has been referred to as Brown II. The complexities of dismantling dual systems included problems related to school plants, transportation of students, personnel, revision of districts and attendance areas, and revision of local laws and regulations. Local school officials, the Court felt, would know best how to accomplish these tasks. The timeline established by the Court read: "With all deliberate speed."

If noncompliance occurred, individuals had the right to seek relief in federal courts. Hundreds of cases have followed since 1954. The Civil Rights Act of 1964 found the federal government taking a stronger stance on desegregation.

CONCLUSION

We have come so far.
We have so far to go!
And miles to go before we sleep.
And miles to go before we sleep.

ENGLE V. VITALE (1962)

SCHOOL DISTRICT OF ABINGTON TOWNSHIP V. SCHEMPP (1963)

ENGEL V. VITALE

Does the reading of a nondenominational prayer at the start of the school day violate the "establishment of religion" clause of the First Amendment?

Yes.

Neither the prayer's nondenominational character nor its voluntary character saves it from unconstitutionality.
~ OYEZ

RELIGION IN COLONIAL AMERICA

Many of the early groups arriving in America came seeking religious freedom. Once acquired, the general practice was for them to deny that same religious freedom to others. Persecution of Quakers, Jews, and Catholics was common, particularly in New England. Official churches were established in some colonies. The Anglican Church in the South and the Congregational Church in New England were adopted as official churches. As shared by Mountjoy, each of the colonies "served as a defender of a particular religious sect." At the time of the Revolution, the Anglican Church was the official church of Maryland, Virginia, North Carolina, and South Carolina. The Congregational Church was the official church of Massachusetts, New

Hampshire, and Connecticut. Georgia, New Jersey, Maryland, and New York experienced the waxing and waning of several religious groups vying for control. Rhode Island, Pennsylvania, and Delaware never declared any of the various churches in their states as an official church.

In states that had an "official religion," citizens were required to pay a "tithing tax" of 10 percent to support their locally established church. Citizens could attend wherever they desired–or not attend if they so desired–but they were still required to pay the tax. During the Revolutionary War, restrictions and biases for or against specific religious groups and individual citizens disappeared in an effort to unite everyone to fight against the common enemy–the British.

RELIGION IN THE UNITED STATES

With the conclusion of the war for independence, the leaders of the young country turned their efforts to the development of a constitution that would determine how the nation would be governed. The 55 representatives to the Constitutional Convention were solidly in support of the concepts that there should be freedom of religion and no one sect should be shown favor over another. Conditional on their approval of the new Constitution, some states required an inclusion of personal rights. Thus, the Bill of Rights was added to the Constitution.

The First Amendment addressed religious freedom and the government. *Congress shall make no law respecting an Establishment of religion, or prohibiting the free exercise thereof. . . .*

Believing as most of the Founding Fathers did that no entanglement should exist between the government and religion, in 1802, Thomas Jefferson wrote to the Danbury Baptists that a wall of separation exists between the church and the state. The original intent was that the wall was to protect the church from the government's interfering in church business. While the government and religion were to remain separated for the next 175 years, Pennsylvania public school students began their day hearing ten or more verses read from the King James Bible and saying the Lord's Prayer followed by the Pledge of Allegiance. The sequence of opening activities was endorsed by many state departments of education throughout the country.

THE NEW YORK PLAN

In 1951, the 22-word prayer developed by the New York State Board of Regents became the focus of a lawsuit that was to change forever the opening exercises of public schools in the United States of America. According to their website, the New York State Regents "are responsible for the general supervision of all educational activities within the State, presiding over The University and the New York State Education Department." The seventeen members of this board were appointed by the state legislature and served in a voluntary capacity. In 1951, the Board of Regents created a "nonsectarian" prayer and sent it to all state schools along with a policy statement to explain its recommended use.

Almighty God, we acknowledge our dependence upon Thee, and we beg Thy blessings upon us, our parents, our teachers and our Country.

According to historian Shane Mountjoy: The policy *"asserted that the American people have always been religious" and "that a program of religious inspiration in the schools" helped accomplish other educational goals. These goals included "respect for authority and obedience to law," so that "each of them will be properly prepared to follow the faith of his or her father, as he or she receives the same at mother's knee or father's side and as such faith is expounded and strengthened by his or her religious leaders."*

Use of the prayer was voluntary, and no district was required to implement the prayer. Those that did use it were to have teachers lead their students in reciting the Pledge of Allegiance followed by the prayer. The prayer was looked upon as nondenominational and, therefore, not considered to be a problem for any child from any religious background. Some persons even referred to it as a "generic prayer" containing no particular theological focus. The prayer received many reactions, some positive and some negative. The American Jewish Congress interpreted it as "too Christian." Opposing the prayer for a variety of reasons were the American Civil Liberties Union, the Citizens Union, the New York Teachers Guild, and the United Parents Association.

Mary Harte, a member of the Board in the Hyde Park School District, suggested that the Board adopt the prayer for their schools. The prayer was eventually put into place in 1958, and it became part of the opening of each school day for the students. Most of the children in the school district were from predominantly Christian faiths. All children were given three options:
- Recite the prayer with the other children.
- Stand silently in the room.
- Be excused from the room and stand in the hall.

ROTH REACTION

As a parent, Lawrence Roth did not like the fact that the district implemented this procedure and that his sons had to make one of the three choices. Roth decided that his sons would not remain in the room during the reciting of the prayer. Once the Roth children began to leave the room during the prayer, other children began to tease them. In addition, since Roth felt that teachers were viewing his sons as troublemakers and harassing them, he decided to take action. He contacted the ACLU, and they agreed to help. It was Roth's belief–supported by the ACLU–that the practice was a violation of the First Amendment: *Congress shall make no law respecting an establishment of religion, or prohibiting the free exercise thereof. . . .*

Under the Establishment Clause, neither a state nor the federal government can set up a church, can pass laws which aid one religion over another, aid all religions, or prefer one religion over others.

Under the Free Exercise Clause, the First Amendment protects the individual against governmental compulsion in religious matters. The state may not interfere with a person's religious observations unless they are a danger to others or to the state. The state may not require a person to take an oath requiring a belief in God in order to qualify for governmental employment.

Next, Roth put an advertisement in the local newspaper that read:
Notice: To all Herrick's school district taxpayers: A taxpayers suit will soon be started to challenge the legality of prayers in public schools. Counsel has been appointed.

All interested parties CALL:

Lawrence Roth
MAYFIAR [sic] 1-7652 /AFTER 5 P.M. DAILY

According to historian Mountjoy, originally approximately 50 persons responded to Roth's ad and agreed to participate in the suit. When everything was said and done, a lot more was said than done. Only five parents ultimately participated. In addition to Roth, Leonore Lyons, David Litchenstein, Monroe Lerner, and Steven Engel took up the cause. Because courts list multiple plaintiffs in alphabetical order, Steven Engel was listed first, thus, giving his name to the case. The respondent of the case was William Vitale, president of the local school board.

GOING TO COURT

The first round of court hearings was held in Nassau County, New York. The lawyer selected by the ACLU to represent the parents was William Butler, a Catholic, in order to make it appear that "he was defending prayer, not attacking it." Judge Bernard S. Meyer listened to both sides presenting their respective cases and then decided for the school district. His reasoning was that as long as the prayer was not compulsory, there was no constitutional violation of the "establishment clause." Judge Meyer added that it was the responsibility of the school district to safeguard the rights of those students who chose not to participate, alluding to protecting the dissenters from harassment.

THE APPEAL

The court of appeals is the highest court in the state of New York. In 1961, the parents appealed their case to the court of appeals, and seven of the nine judges affirmed the decision of the lower court. Two of the judges opined that the prayer was unconstitutional and would erode "the mighty bulwark erected by the First Amendment."

The Chief Justice writing for the majority stated:
Saying this simple prayer may be, according to the broadest possible dictionary definition, an act of "religion," but when the Founding Fathers prohibited "an establishment of religion" they were referring to official adoption of, or favor to, one or more sects.

THE SUPREME COURT

If the Supreme Court opts to hear a case, a **writ of certiorari** is issued, and all courts that have previously heard the case send their records to the United States Supreme Court. On December 4, 1961, the Court issued the writ, briefs were submitted by both sides, and oral arguments were heard on April 3, 1962. While the Supreme Court hears arguments from both the petitioner (the parents) and the respondent (the school district), other persons may file a brief. These persons are known as **amicus curiae**, or "friends of the court." As reported by Mountjoy, the Attorneys General from 22 states filed briefs supporting the prayer, while the American Ethical Union, the American Jewish Committee, and the Synagogue Council of America each filed briefs opposing the prayer.

Earl Warren, the Chief Justice of the Supreme Court, was appointed by President Eisenhower in 1953, a decision that

Eisenhower reportedly later regretted. The Court under Warren has the reputation of being the most liberal Court in the nation's history. The Associate Justices in 1962: Hugo Black; William Brennan, Jr.; Tom Clark; William Douglas; Felix Frankfurter; John Harlan; Potter Stewart; and Byron White. This was essentially the same Court that had heard and decided *Brown v. the Board of Education, Miranda v. Arizona,* and several cases involving voter rights in the early 1960s. Justice White ultimately did not participate in the *Engel* decision since he had not yet been confirmed.

The question that the Court had to answer was simple: Does a school-sponsored, nondenominational prayer in public schools violate the Establishment Clause of the First Amendment?

The answer: Yes.

THE DECISION

Justice Hugo Black, writing for the majority, stated that having a school-sponsored prayer was in violation of the Constitution. For precedent, Black cited wars, persecutions, and other destructive events that had occurred when government became involved in religious affairs. Black, still writing for the majority, declared that the First Amendment's purpose was to prevent government interference with religion. Summarizing the point, Black wrote that since Americans follow a wide variety of religious creeds, it is not appropriate for the government to endorse any one belief over another.

The one dissenting vote was submitted by Justice Potter Stewart who argued that the Establishment Clause's only purpose was to prevent a state-sponsored church as is done in Great Britain with the Church of England. He saw the nondenominational nature of the prayer and the opportunity for students to not participate adequate.

THE AFTERMATH

Reaction to the *Engel* decision was swift and widespread. The United States Supreme Court "kicked God out of the schools," became a new catchphrase. Nearly six decades later, the *Engel* decision is reviled as one that put America "on the road to moral decay," and in the words of one writer has been "linked to every social ill from schoolhouse shootings to drug addiction." Using the *Engel* decision, advocacy groups raise millions of dollars every year. Senator Sam Ervin of North Carolina said, "The Supreme Court has made God unconstitutional."

One Georgian member of Congress complained that the Supreme Court "put Negroes in the schools–now they put God out of the schools!" The bottom line, however, is that *Engel* did not make praying in schools illegal. *Engel* declared that it could not be a school-led prayer.

As Charles C. Haynes, senior scholar at the First Amendment Center, has challenged: "Visit most public schools today and you are likely to see students praying around the flagpole, attending religious club meetings, giving each other religious literature, saying grace before lunch, talking about their faith in class discussions and in other ways expressing their religious convictions."

ABINGTON V. SCHEMPP (1963)

Does reading the Bible in public school classrooms each morning violate the religious freedom of students as provided by the First and Fourteenth Amendments?

Yes.

The required activities encroached on both the Free Exercise Clause and the Establishment Clause of the First Amendment since the readings and recitations were essentially religious ceremonies and were "intended by the State to be so."

~ OYEZ

At the time of the Abington case, Pennsylvania was one of four states that required daily Bible reading at the beginning of each day. Twenty-five other states gave schools the option of Bible reading, and courts had already struck down Bible reading in eleven other states. At the beginning of the school day, all Pennsylvania public school students heard a minimum of ten verses read from the Bible followed by their reciting the Lord's Prayer. Abington School District complied with this requirement.

Ellery Schempp was a high school junior at Abington High School in 1956 when the administration decided to broadcast the opening exercises over the public address system. They included reading from the Bible (without comment), followed by students rising, reciting the Lord's Prayer, and saying the Pledge of Allegiance. One morning, Schempp protested the practice by remaining seated and reading silently from the *Quran*. While the Schempp family were Unitarians, Ellery felt that the religious exercises also offended his Jewish classmates. Ellery said that he chose the *Quran* only because it was one of his father's books. As a consequence of his protest, Ellery was assigned to the guidance counselor's office during the homeroom period for the remainder of the school year. Ellery's father, Edward Schempp, sued the school district to enjoin further Bible reading.

DISTRICT COURT

During the district court trial, expert witnesses spoke for both sides. While a rabbi testified that reading from the New Testament does harm to Jewish children, one of the co-founders of the National Council of Churches testified that the Bible does not favor any Christian sect and that eliminating the New Testament would discriminate against Christianity. The federal district court found for the Schempps, and Abington Township School District appealed to the United States Supreme Court.

Since Pennsylvania then altered its law by excusing students from the exercise upon parental request, the Supreme Court threw out the earlier decision and sent it back to district court. Schempp again sued the school district and again the district court found for the plaintiff. Again, the school district appealed the decision, and the Supreme Court agreed to hear the case.

THE SUPREME COURT

The *Schempp* case was combined with *Murray v. Curlett*, a case from Baltimore, Maryland. This case included William Murray, the son of Madalyn Murray O'Hair, the founder of the American Atheists organization.

The Court was the same Court that had heard *Engel v. Vitale* a year earlier. The attorney for the school district argued that the purpose of the Pennsylvania law was to teach morality, not religion. The attorney for the Schempps countered by stating, "You cannot separate the moral leaven from the religious leaven in the Bible." In other words, one cannot separate the moral teachings of the Bible from the religious teachings.

THE DECISION

On June 17, 1963, the United States Supreme Court found for Schempp by a vote of 8 to 1. Justice Tom C. Clark delivered the majority opinion. Clark summarized many of the points made in the *Engel v. Vitale* decision and expanded some of the others that reading the Bible in public school classrooms each morning violates the religious freedom of students. In its ruling, the Court wanted to ensure that not only does the state not promote a particular religion, but also it does not promote all religions or religion generally. In essence, the government is to maintain a level of neutrality in regard to religion. The Schempp case was especially significant since it established what is known as the "secular purpose" and the "primary effect" tests for cases dealing with the Establishment Clause. If either the purpose or the effect of government action is to advance or inhibit religion, the action is unconstitutional.

THE DISSENT

Again, as in *Engel v. Vitale,* Justice Potter Stewart was the one dissenting opinion. Stewart's stance was that if schools prohibited Bible reading, they are no longer neutral regarding religion.

THE AFTERMATH

In both the *Engel* and the *Abington* cases, the persons raising the concern received a large amount of hate mail and death threats, were harassed and threatened, and experienced acts of violence against their homes. Newspaper articles and editorials followed.

IN CONCLUSION

Both *Engel v. Vitale* and *Abington v. Schempp* clarified Jefferson's "wall of separation" that needs to exist between church and state.

As pointed out by Haynes, however, both *Engel v. Vitale* and *Abington v. Schempp* paradoxically enabled religion and religious practices to play a larger role in schools than at anytime since the nineteenth century. **"Schempp became the founding document for teaching about religion in public school."** As writer historian Matthew Brown posited: *Schempp . . . clarified that while government can't promote or denigrate religion, the subject of faith and its role in history, literature and the arts has educational value and can be taught in public schools.*

In the words of English Poet William Cowper:

The Lord moves in a mysterious way,
his wonders to perform.

UNITED STATES V. NIXON (1974)

Is the President's right to safeguard certain information, using his "executive privilege" confidentiality power entirely immune from judicial review?

No.

Neither the doctrine of separation of powers, nor the generalized need for confidentiality of high-level communications, without more, can sustain an absolute, unqualified, presidential privilege.

~ OYEZ

INTRODUCTION

On November 5, 1968, Richard M. Nixon was elected to his first term as President of the United States, defeating Hubert H. Humphrey by little more than 500,000 votes. In his victory speech, the President-elect assured the nation that his goal was to bring a divided country together:

This will be an open administration, open to new ideas, open to men and women of both parties, open to the critics as well as those who support us. We want to bridge the generation gap. We want to bridge the gap between races. We want to bring America together.

THE FIRST TERM

The major problem confronting the new President was the same problem that had frustrated his predecessor–the war in Vietnam. A major part of his election campaign had been based on the promise to end the war in Southeast Asia and bring the troops home. Once in office, Nixon found the promise not so easy to fulfill. Also, once in office, the promise of the administration's being "open" was abandoned, and secrecy became the standard operating procedure in the White House. The bombing of North Vietnamese camps in Cambodia became classified information until the *New York Times* learned of it and published articles about it.

As the war continued in Vietnam, the number of demonstrations opposing the war continued to rise at home. In May of 1970, student protestors from Kent State University were demonstrating against the continued bombings. Ohio National Guard troops met the student demonstrators at Kent State, and shots were fired into the crowd of protestors. Four students were killed.

During the second half of his first term, Nixon acted to do what he referred to as "Vietnamizing" the war, which meant turning the fighting over to the Vietnamese. As election time approached in 1972, U.S. combat forces had been reduced from 543,000 in 1969 to 32,200. Nixon seemed to always feel under attack, and he steeled himself by not trusting anyone. "We were obsessed with secrecy. As a matter of fact, I was paranoiac or almost a basket case with regard to secrecy," he later admitted. He appeared to be wary always.

THE 1972 CAMPAIGN

As the presidential election of 1972 approached, the Democrats were a divided party. Four candidates had initially announced their candidacies: Edward Kennedy, Edmund Muskie, and Hubert Humphrey–all U.S. Senators– and South Dakota Senator George McGovern. Three of the

Democratic candidates eventually withdrew for a variety of reasons. Kennedy said that he had decided to remain in the Senate. Muskie and Humphrey had not done well in the primaries. That left McGovern, probably the weakest of the four candidates.

Nixon spent more money on the 1972 campaign than had any candidate in United States history, but he was still concerned that he might lose. Then, on October 26, Henry Kissinger, the President's negotiator in Vietnam, announced, "Peace is at hand." The election was nearly a "no contest." Nixon received 60.7 percent of the popular vote and 520 electoral votes. It appeared that his worries were over. HOWEVER . . .

THE BURGLARY

Five months before the election victory, Democratic National Committee headquarters housed in the Watergate Hotel at the intersection of Virginia and New Hampshire avenues had been broken into. In the process of what Nixon's press secretary Ron Ziegler referred to as a "third-rate burglary," the five perpetrators had been caught and arrested because of an alert security guard. The five men arrested were Virgilio Gonzalez, Bernard Barker, James McCord, Eugenio Martínez, and Frank Sturgis. They were charged with attempted burglary and attempted interception of telephone and other communications. The burglars' address books contained names and phone numbers. Among the names was E. Howard Hunt.

The burglary was planned by an organization nicknamed "the White House Plumbers." Their job–leaks. Primary operatives in the planning of the burglary were G. Gordon Liddy and E. Howard Hunt. Both had been hired by Egil

Krogh. Liddy, a former member of the Federal Bureau of Investigation, was appointed Staff Assistant to the President of the United States in 1971. Hunt, a former member of the Central Intelligence Agency, was hired in 1971 as a public relations consultant. In 1971, Hunt and Liddy had recommended a break-in of the office of Dr. Lewis Fielding, the psychiatrist of Daniel Ellsberg, hoping to get information to discredit Ellsberg who had released the Pentagon Papers. Assistant to the President John Ehrlichman gave approval of the burglary as long as it was not traceable to the White House.

The day after the burglary, G. Gordon Liddy told Attorney General Richard Kleindienst that the operation had begun in the White House and that he should arrange to have the burglars released. Although he did not do so, Kleindienst also did not report Liddy's comments. Kleindienst had been initially appointed Deputy Attorney General. When Attorney General John Mitchell resigned to head Nixon's reelection campaign, Nixon promoted Kleindienst to the top slot. Frederick LaRue, an aide to the President without title, also worked with the reelection campaign. In an attempt to buy silence, LaRue paid $300,000 in hush money. The money was given to Hunt's wife Dorothy for distribution.

Dorothy Hunt was killed in the crash of United Airlines Flight 533 at Midway Airport in Chicago on December 8, 1972. An interesting sidelight regarding Dorothy Hunt is that she was upset about an interruption in the payments to silence the Watergate defendants. Allegedly, she threatened to go to the press regarding information that she had indicating that Nixon was involved in the FBI/CIA murder of President Kennedy. Television newsperson Michele Clark was in the process of interviewing Hunt and died with her when the plane crashed in Chicago.

The burglars pleaded guilty in a trial presided over by John Sirica, and they were sentenced. G. Gordon Liddy and James McCord pled not guilty but were found guilty and sentenced to long terms in prison.

THE PLOT THICKENS

During the trial for Liddy and McCord, former treasurer for the Committee to Reelect the President (CREEP), knew about a payment of $199,000 that he was told to give to Liddy. While he said that he had no idea what Liddy did with the money, former Attorney General and former Commerce Secretary Maurice Stans knew about the payment. This testimony tied the burglary to the Nixon administration. In early February, the Senate voted 70-0 to establish a seven-member committee to investigate Watergate. North Carolina Senator Sam Ervin was named to chair the committee. Serving on the committee in addition to Ervin: Democrats Daniel Inouye, Hawaii; Joseph Montoya, New Mexico; and Herman Tallmadge, Georgia; and Republicans Howard Baker, Tennessee; Edward Gurney, Florida; and Lowell Weicker, Connecticut.

Nixon's response at the time to the investigation:
When I heard about the forced entry and bugging, I thought, What [. . .] is this? What is the matter with these people? Are they crazy? I thought they were nuts! A prank! I think our Democratic friends know that, too, [although] they think I have people capable of it. And they are correct.
. . . Then Nixon offered: *But let's remember this was not done by the White House. This was done by the Committee to Re-elect, and [John] Mitchell was the Chairman. . . . Mitchell won't allow himself to be ruined. He will put on his big stone face.*

Historian D. J. Herda wrote that Nixon believed that the Senate committee would not be content with just sending the burglars to jail. "They wanted the burglars to identify participants higher up in the Nixon administration, and they would use any means they could to accomplish this."

On March 19, 1973, James McCord, one of the burglars, sent a letter to Judge Sirica. In the letter, he indicated that some of the defendants had lied in court and that members of the Nixon administration were paying defendants to remain silent and to cover everything up. On April 30, 1973, President Nixon went on national television and announced the resignations of John Ehrlichman and Bob Haldeman, his two special aides. He also indicated that White House counsel John Dean had been dismissed.

THE HEARINGS

On June 26, 1973, John Dean was called to testify at the hearing. His testimony was cataclysmic for the President. He swore under oath: Nixon had lied to the nation. Nixon had known about the cover up since at least September of 1972. Nixon kept an "enemies list" containing hundreds of names. Dean testified that the enemy's list was used to harass people through illegal investigation into their tax information and other ways. Not all of the persons were politicians, since many of the members of the media and popular actors and actresses were on this list.

The person credited with compiling the enemies list was special counsel to the President Charles "Chuck" Colson who had led Nixon's campaign in 1972. Colson said that he would "walk over my own grandmother to get the President reelected."

On July 13, 1973, former White House aide Alexander Butterfield was called to testify before the Committee. Butterfield shared that Nixon had a voice-activated recording system installed in the Oval Office to tape all of his conversations. When the committee requested that the President turn over some of the tapes to them, Nixon refused, claiming executive privilege. Attorney General Elliot Richardson appointed Archibald Cox as the special prosecutor to investigate the case. Cox subpoenaed the tapes that the committee wanted to review, and again Nixon refused. Cox then took the case to Judge Sirica, and the judge upheld the special prosecutor's demand.

Simultaneously, Spiro Agnew, Nixon's Vice President, was forced to resign when federal attorneys were able to prove that he had taken bribes both during his years as Governor of Maryland and during his first term as Vice President. Needing a highly respected individual to replace Agnew, Nixon nominated Gerald Ford from Michigan. The Senate quickly confirmed the appointment.

SATURDAY NIGHT MASSACRE

As the hearings continued, on October 20, the President ordered Attorney General Richardson to fire Archibald Cox, the Special Prosecutor, since Cox was still pursuing the tapes that Nixon would not release. Rather than fire Cox, Richardson resigned. Serving under Richardson was Deputy Attorney General William Ruckelshaus, whom Nixon then directed to fire Cox. Rather than fire Cox, Ruckelshaus resigned. Eventually, Nixon found someone to fire Cox. It was Robert Bork, the solicitor general. Nixon made Bork acting attorney general, and Bork fired Cox, abolishing the position.

NIXON'S PLAN

Six months later, President Nixon developed a new plan to relieve the pressure that he was under. He reestablished the office of special prosecutor to investigate Watergate and appointed Leon Jaworski to continue the investigation. In an effort to alleviate the mounting pressures, Nixon offered to release typed transcripts of the requested tapes. The 1,216 pages of transcripts were found to have significant gaps and redactions. Jaworski did not accept the transcripts as an appropriate response by the President to the request to provide the tapes. When Nixon still refused to submit the tapes, Jaworski petitioned the United States Supreme Court to decide on *United States v. Nixon.*

UNITED STATES V. NIXON

On July 8, 1974, the Supreme Court heard arguments from Special Prosecutor Jaworski regarding the Court's jurisdiction to hear the case. Following interaction with Jaworski and being informed about the President's claim of executive privilege, the Court decided that it did have jurisdiction to hear the case.

As delineated by historian D. J. Herda, Jaworski had three questions for the Court.

- Does the Supreme Court have jurisdiction over the case?
- Does the Court have the authority to decide whether or not executive privilege exists, even though not mentioned in the Constitution?
- If executive privilege exists, under what circumstances may the President apply it?

After Jaworski's opening remarks, James D. St. Clair provided his opening statements on behalf of the President. St. Clair's argument was that the issue was not "executive privilege" but whether the Court should hear the case since their doing so might impact upon the House Judiciary Committee's hearings on the impeachment of the President. St. Clair's interaction with the Court was weak, and the Justices did not receive the definitive answers they wanted. In regard to the matter of "executive privilege," St. Clair said that the President believed it was absolute. "The President wants me to argue that he is as powerful a monarch as Louis XIV, only four years at a time, and is not subject to the processes of any court in the land except the court of impeachment."

THE COURT'S DECISION

The Supreme Court did not agree with St. Clair's argument. The Court ruled that **the President is not above the law and must comply with subpoenas like any other citizen. Executive privilege exists based only on military or national security issues.**

NIXON COMPLIES

Nixon knew that "the smoking gun," as it was called, was among the tapes and that impeachment would result. As required, however, less than a week later, the tapes were turned over to Special Prosecutor Jaworski. On August 8, 1974, knowing that the tapes would provide the evidence that would result in his impeachment and eventual removal from office, Nixon announced his resignation effective at noon on August 9. He told the nation: "I have never been a quitter. To leave office before my term is completed is abhorrent to every instinct in my body. But as President I must put the interests of America first." He closed his address with a prayer: "May God's grace be with you in all the days ahead."

FORD SWORN IN

On August 9, 1974, Gerald Ford was sworn in as President by Chief Justice Warren Burger. In his first address to the nation, President Ford stated: **Our long national nightmare is over. . . . Our Constitution works; our great Republic is a government of laws not of men.**

AFTERMATH

On September 8, 1974, President Ford issued Proclamation 4311. The Proclamation was a full and unconditional pardon for any crimes former President Nixon might have committed against the United States while President. Because of the anger and the animosity that many persons in the country held against former President Nixon, many historians and political analysts believe that the pardon may have cost Ford the opportunity to win the 1976 presidential election.

On January 1, 1975, H.R. Haldeman, John Ehrlichman, and John Mitchell were found guilty of crimes involving Watergate. They were each sentenced to two and one-half to eight years in prison. Ultimately, 40 government officials were indicted or jailed.

IN CONCLUSION

The office of President of the United States as designed and limited by the Constitution is not the equivalent to that of a monarch. The authority associated with the presidency is not absolute, limited by the U.S. Constitution.

CONCLUSION

These six cases have been addressed by the United States Supreme Court. Each decision is a product of its time and of the Justices serving on the Court.

In *Marbury v. Madison,* we learn that the U.S. Supreme Court has the final say for interpreting the Constitution and what authority the Court holds.

In *Dred Scott v. Sandford,* we learn that the politics and the personal attitudes of Supreme Court Justices can foster a bad and unfair decision.

In *Plessy v. Ferguson,* we learn that a decision handed down by the Supreme Court can be affected by the social attitudes of the time.

In *Brown v. Board of Education,* we learn that *separate* is far from *equal*, and the Fourteenth Amendment provides equal protection to all of the country's citizens.

In *Engel v. Vitale* and *Abington v. Schempp,* we learn that the Constitution continuously protects citizens from a forced religiousness and protects religions from governmental interference.

In *United States v. Nixon,* we learn that the President of the United States is not above the law.

Through the study of these six cases, we are reminded of how well constructed the United States Constitution is and how foresighted the drafters were.

U.S. Supreme Court: Six Decisions That Changed America demonstrates "Congress does not have the power to modify the Constitution through regular legislation because the Supremacy Clause places the Constitution before the laws."

THE SUPREME COURT RULED

- The Court has the power to declare a law unconstitutional.
- A negro was not a citizen, had no standing to sue in federal court, declared the Missouri Compromise unconstitutional.
  - Within a decade, this decision was overturned by passage of the Fourteenth Amendment.
- Segregation did not, in itself, constitute unlawful discrimination.
- Segregation of public education based solely on race violates the equal protection clause of the Fourteenth Amendment.
- Neither a prayer's nondenominational character nor its voluntary character saves it from unconstitutionality.
- Bible reading in public school classrooms violates the religious freedom of students as provided by the First and Fourteenth amendments.
- The President has no right to declare certain information immune from judicial review by claiming "executive privilege."

Our Constitution works;
our great Republic is a government of laws not of men.

~ Gerald R. Ford

U.S. Supreme Court: Six Cases That Changed America
MAJOR SOURCES

Axelrod-Contrada, Joan. *Plessy v. Ferguson: Separate But Unequal.* 2009.

Baker, Liva. "With All Deliberate Speed [**Brown v. Board of Education**]," *American Heritage Magazine.*

Bartholomew, Paul C. *Summaries of Leading Cases of the Constitution.* 1965.

Catton, Bruce. "**Dred Scott v. Sandford**: Black Pawn on a Field of Peril," *American Heritage Magazine.*

Cushman, Robert E. *Leading Constitutional Decisions.* 1963.

Feinman, Jay M. *Supreme Court Decisions.* 2012.

Finkelman, Paul. *Dred Scott v. Sandford: A Brief History with Documents.* 1997.

Garraty, John A. "**Marbury v. Madison**: The Case of the Missing Commissions," *American Heritage Magazine.*

Haynes, Charles C., and others. *The First Amendment in Schools.* 2003.

Herda, D.J. *United States v. Nixon: Watergate and the President.* 1996.

Hofstadter, Richard, William Miller, and Daniel Aaron. *The United States: The History of a Republic.* 1957.

Hudgins, H.C., Jr., and Richard S. Vacca. *Law and Education: Contemporary Issues.* 1995.

McCarthy, Martha M. *A Delicate Balance: Church, State, and the Schools.* 1983.

Mountjoy, Shane. *Engel v. Vitale: School Prayer and the Establishment Clause.* 2007.

Patterson, James T. *Brown v. Board of Education: A Civil Rights Milestone and Its Troubled Legacy.* 2001.

Russo, Charles J. *Reutter's The Law of Public Education.* 2004.

Thomas, Brook. *Plessy v. Ferguson: A Brief History with Documents.* 1997.

Trachtman, Michael G. *The Supremes' Greatest Hits: The 44 Supreme Court Cases That Most Directly Affect Your Life.* 2007.

Vacca, Richard S., and H.C. Hudgins, Jr. *The Legacy of the Burger Court and the Schools 1969-1986.* 1991.

Woodward, C. Vann. "**Plessy v. Ferguson**: The Birth of Jim Crow," *American Heritage Magazine.*

Robert A. Frick, Ed.D.

Dr. Robert Frick served 45 years in the Lampeter-Strasburg (PA) School District–three years as an elementary teacher and 42 years as an administrator. The District's first Assistant Superintendent, he spent his last 15 years as Superintendent of Schools.

A graduate of Millersville University of Pennsylvania with both his Bachelor of Science and Master of Science degrees, Dr. Frick holds a Doctorate in Educational Administration from Temple University. He has served as adjunct professor of educational administration for several colleges.

Since retiring, Dr. Frick has been drawn into the world of living history. A guide for Historic Lancaster Walking Tours, he also has prepared numerous one-hour PowerPoint presentations that have been rewritten as prose for publication.

- *Together, They Made Lancaster Great*
  (Volumes I and II)

- *Together, They Made the Modern American Presidency: FDR to George W. Bush*
- *Together, They Made the Modern American First Ladyship: Eleanor Roosevelt to Laura Bush*
  (Volumes I and II)

- *Together, They Founded the United States: Six Founding Fathers*
  (John Jay, Alexander Hamilton, John Adams, Thomas Jefferson, James Madison, and James Monroe)

- *U.S. Supreme Court: Six Decisions That Changed America*
  (*Marbury v. Madison, Dred Scott v. Sandford, Plessy v. Ferguson, Brown v. Board of Education, Engle v. Vitale and School District of Abington Township v. Schempp, United States v. Nixon*)